ARBATEL WORKINGS

Meditations and Rituals

Suba

ISBN: 978-0-9851672-6-4

CONTENTS

	INTRODUCTION	5
I	SEVEN AXIOMS	7
II	RITUAL WORKINGS	11
III	PLANETARY CORRESPONDENCES	37
IV	RITUALS	55
V	APHORISMS	129
VI	RANDOM THOUGHTS	175
	REFERENCES	179
	INDEX	181
	ABOUT THE AUTHOR	

BLESSINGS

INTRODUCTION

This is a record of my meditations, rituals, practices and things that have arisen through my work with the Arbatel. This is a practitioner's journal. In saying, while I have made the effort to stay true to the Arbatel's goals, in the end, this work is an integration of the Arbatel system into my own energetic framework, and so, it obviously reflects my philosophies, beliefs and understandings.

I highly suggest you buy a copy of the Arbatel so that you have the source text to work with. Then, once you have attained some skill in working with the grimoire you can reflect, compare and contrast your experiences with mine. It is my hope this journal will support and inspire you. The most complete and authoritative translation of the Arbatel in English is Joseph Petersons, *Arbatel: Concerning the Magic of the Ancients.*

To me the Arbatel shares with the reader a way of life and a way of commencing and undertaking the journey towards manifesting their Will. It guides us to our Highest Conception of Self and then towards its embodiment within our daily lives.

The Arbatel introduces us to the celestial planes of the Mind and Universe, giving us the keys to open those doors and the knowledge to work with the celestial energies in a safe and respectful way. It is one of the few grimoires that focuses on positivity, joyfulness, uplifting, brightening, enriching, compassion and Theurgia.

The Arbatel offers us a systematic Path of Development: from Adepthood (mastering the bodily energies) to becoming a Master Adept who controls the Elemental energies, and then to a Great Adept who's touched the Heavens and entered into deeper and more encompassing levels of Being and Communion. Through this process we transcend/dissolve/look beyond the ego as we enter Theurgia (Oneness).

The Arbatel is filled with guidance towards inner contentment and joyfulness. Within its pages are many aphorisms pointing to energetic conservation, refinement and expression, while instructing us to enjoy Life as we embrace and grow from our experiences.

Unlike other grimoires which seek to externally dominate, manipulate, bribe, force, or in some way influence the spiritual realms, the Arbatel has us embody the energies through first gaining a relationship with the Olympic Spirits, touching in and learning from them, before ultimately integrating their essences and energies into our lives to do with as we wish. Once we understand and know how to work with the spirits' energies, we no longer need to call upon them.

While I have made the effort to create a complete text, in that, you have all the necessary ingredients to work with the Olympic Spirits in a safe and empowering way, I still highly suggest you acquire a copy of the Arbatel. In no way do I want you to blindly follow my system. In fact, I encourage you to create your own.

The first chapter in *Arbatel Workings* focuses on the Seven Axioms, which are the condensed teachings I gained while meditating on the 49 Aphorisms.

The next chapter focuses on Ritual Workings: laying out the basic tools, processes, and means to fully benefit from the Arbatel while introducing us to the Olympic Spirits (Energies and Intelligences of the Planetary Spheres).

Following Ritual Workings is a chapter on Planetary Correspondences that offers a descent, but by no means exhaustive treatment on the planetary energies.

The fourth chapter offers my insights, experiences, and practices that I gained while invoking the Olympic Spirits and working with their energies: both individually and together.

Chapter five expounds upon the Seven Axioms with the complete pithy poems and insights that arose from my meditations on the 49 Aphorisms.

The last chapter offers a few Random Thoughts and experiences I had while working with the Arbatel.

May you find something of value in my words and may you be Blessed with all the gifts of Life.

Suba

SEVEN AXIOMS

Know and Act Accordingly 7
Know Self 7
Be Self 8
Through Self, Truth is Known .. 8
Know the Truth 8
Embody the Truth 8
Be Fulfilled 9

Know and Act Accordingly

Be fully present, use discernment, find your ground, your balance, and be receptive to the energies. Come to know yourself, be your Highest Concept of Self and Enjoy your Life. Be truthful to who you are, avoid those energies that take you away from Self and attract those energies that support your efforts towards Embodying Your Truth.

Be open and don't waste your time and energy. Be patience, loving, kind, compassionate and wise. Transform those energies of hate, anger, fear, boredom, sadness, ignorance, depleting desires, and being locked down/attached, with love, patience, trust, embodiment, joyfulness, knowledge, conscious manifestation and openness. Conserve your energy, reflect and grow.

Listen and Trust. Create the world you desire and enjoy yourself. Everything in Life is Divine: each offering an energy pattern/frequency of Life – like many rivulets coming from one source and flowing to the Oceanic Oneness of B-ing.

Be ever watchful: allow only those energies you seek for to be in your life – let the rest go. Have intentional focus while inspecting the mind and body to see how the energies affect/effect it. Keep your focus on Kether, embody Self in Malkut, and awaken through Tiphareth.

Know Self

Let all doubts dissolve like wax from Truth's Flame:
Believe in Your Truth, Take Refuge in Your Truth, Be Your Truth.

Learn to Listen.
Know the voice through contemplation,
meditation,
and discernment:

know the energy's consequences/effects.

Know what you want.
Know what invites that and what doesn't
and then act accordingly.

Be Self

Know the Source of Energy. Then find a system that accords with your temperament/circumstances and use it to tap into that energy; invoke those energies you seek for in life and learn to control and embody them.

Learn about the different ways to work with those energies and then create the reality you wish. Just be aware, beware, of those things that take you away from your Truth/Self. And, as with all things, be thankful, respectful, kind and loving.

Through Self, Truth is Known

Master the bodily and elemental energies before touching in with the celestial energies. In other words, master the body's chi/prana, master the elemental planes, and then the celestial ones. Know the validity of each energy and use it towards accomplishing your aims.

Be content in all that you do; find everything you need within yourself. Don't be attached to any one thing, state, power, insight, or what have you. Learn to listen to all the different dimensions of your Being, finding your center through constant Practice/Embodiment. Align yourself to your Highest Truth and allow its Grace/Light to shine within you.

Know the Truth

Know your Power, be fully Present with what is, and invite those energies you seek for in your life. Conserve your energy while using the tools that you have to accomplish your aims. Perceive from the multidimensional realms while residing within the physical plane. Seek to connect all dimensions of Self 2-gether. Unify the Self and B Whole.

Embody the Truth

Through the process of Theurgy (inviting energies within ourselves) we come to know the order, form, and mode of those things we work with. Through that experience we gain the knowledge and means towards working with their energies directly, no longer needing the intelligences to be present, for we now radiate it ourselves.

Gaining the ability to work with these energies does not mean we have mastered ourselves. We must process the experiences, insights, practices, and apply them in our daily lives. Only then will our perspective change, and with our perspective, the energies of our lives. So always use discretion, be mindful, gain knowledge and through reflection, understand, and through understanding, integrate those energies into your life and become wiser through them.

Contemplate, look inside and take account, know yourself, be diligent in your quest, never give up, trust in yourself and be Open.

Fulfillment

We seek Complete Fulfillment. Through the stages of Adepthood to becoming a Master Adept and then a Great One, we embody the Divine Qualities of an Awaken Self:
Constantly Blessing – Eternally Blessed.

RITUAL WORKINGS

Planetary Hours ..	11
Sigils	14
Mantras	21
Incense	27
Rituals	32
Spirits	34

Planetary Hours

There are a lot of factors that go into a successful ritual. One factor is timing. Traditionally there are three things to take into consideration when we work with time: (1) the month, day, and hour we undertake our rituals; (2) current cycle, position and aspect of the planets; (3) and the planetary transits to our birth chart. When we can align all three considerations in our rituals, we have optimized the timing of our undertakings.

While there is no guarantee that timing alone will determine our success, it does, at the very least, increase the odds of it doing so.

There are two different planetary hour systems that I know of. Both of them start with the rising sun. Depending on the day will determine which planet rules the first hour of the day.

The traditional assignments of planets to days are:

Sun	–	Sunday
Moon	–	Monday
Mars	–	Tuesday
Mercury	–	Wednesday
Jupiter	–	Thursday
Venus	–	Friday
Saturn	–	Saturday

If you are doing a ritual on Sunday, then the first hour will be ruled by the Sun.

Two Planetary Hour Systems

The difference between the two systems comes after the first hour. Traditionally every hour is ruled by a different planet or luminary. Starting on Sunday, the first hour would be ruled by the Sun, the next hour by Venus then Mercury, Moon, Saturn, Jupiter, Mars, and then the Sun again. The cycle repeats throughout the day ending on Mercury's hour. The sunrise the next day starts with the Moon on Monday and so on throughout the whole week. Each day starting with the planet that rules that day.

Unlike the traditional planetary hour system, the second system uses unequal stations. In other words, while the traditional system goes by the hour, the newer system determines the length of day and night according to the actual number of hours the sun is above the horizon.

For example, let us say the day is 16 hours long while the night is 8 hours long. By dividing 16 hours or 960 minutes by 12, each planet in the day will rule 80 minutes. By dividing 480 minutes by 12, we determine that each planet will rule for 40 minutes during the night hours. The order in which the planets rule is the same as the traditional system, the only difference is the length of time they rule.

Both systems work. Though, I do tend to work with the second, as it takes into account the differences between night and day throughout the year.

As to when the planetary hours were first introduced, we know for certain that it goes back to the early Grecian times, though, there are many who believe it first arose with the ancient Babylonians.

As to why the planets rule the days, I have come across four different theories.

The first theory has us set our intention on Sunday as we plant the seeds we wish to manifest during the week.

Then we align our sub/unconscious drives with our conscious ones on Monday (Moon).We ignite the energy and Will it forth on Tuesday (Mars). Burning and overcoming all obstacles, we direct the energy to what and where we want the energy to go on Wednesday (Mercury). Expanding and manifesting our intentions on Thursday (Jupiter) and then integrating and enjoying the fruits of our labors on Friday (Venus).

On Saturday (Saturn) we reflect, solidify and relax, before beginning another week.

A second theory I have heard is the beginning of life:

Gestation (Moon)
Multiplication (Mars)
Specializing (Mercury)
Growing (Jupiter)
Refining (Venus)
Death via the birth canal (Saturn)
to the sun's light:

A Baby (Sun)

A third possibility revolves around commerce and business:

Conceiving an idea on Sunday
Working through any problems on Monday
Willing it into being on Tuesday
Negotiating and tweaking things on Wednesday
Coming to an agreement on Thursday
Celebrating the fruition of our labors on Friday
Resting and enjoying our lives on Saturday

A fourth explanation is related to gardening:

Planting the seeds on Sunday
Rooting on Monday
Sprouting on Tuesday
Spreading leaves on Wednesday
Flowering on Thursday
Fruiting on Friday
and Harvesting on Saturday.

I am not sure what plant grows from seed to fruit in a week, but it must be a cool one. Maybe magic shrums?

Working with the Hours and Days

One facet of working with the planetary hours that I have found to be fruitful is to calculate when, within the planetary hour we are working with, what the most beneficial time to start the ritual is. George Llewellyn suggests that we start our endeavors at least a few minutes after the start of the planet's hour. This insures that we are in fact, fully within the hour of the planetary energy.

Some say that we should not begin a ritual during the waning time of the hour. In other words, if the planet rules an hour, then we should start our ritual before the halfway mark (30 minutes). After that time, the planet's energy starts to wane and shift to the next energy. I personally have not noticed a difference, but maybe you will – so pay attention. It would seem fitting to start a ritual during a planet's waning time if we were seeking to rid ourselves and overcome unwanted aspects of that planet's sphere.

A third aspect of working with the planetary hours is to numerologically add up the minutes to determine the Root Number. When we find a time that equals a Planet's Root Number according to the Kabbalah, we have found, like a cell phone signal, a stronger connection.

Let's say we wish to work with the Sun on Jupiter's day. We would want to commence our activities at 17:43 = 8:7 = 15 = 6 (this will be different depending on the time of year). The root number equals Tiphareth. This would be a great time to initiate our ritual.

Side Note: Don't get caught up in the hours. They are useful tools in strengthening our rituals and bringing about more awareness in our lives, but by no means are they absolutely necessary. I have had many successful rituals without once considering the time. So relax.

Working with the Planet's Heavenly Position

The second planetary timing has to do with the planet's cycle, position and aspect. The Moon being the easiest to work with. We not only consider its relationship to where it is in the heavens (house and sign), but its actual phase as well (full, half, quarter, new). Working with the moon adds a lot of energy into our rituals. In this particular text I am not going to get into all the details of working with the Moon, as that will be something I will talk about in a later writing.

This works with all the planets. Some have very long cycles: 28-30 years for Saturn, about 12 with Jupiter, close to two for Mars, a little less than two thirds a year for Venus, 88 days for Mercury, and approximately 28 days for the moon. Coordinating the planet's movements with our rituals is a great way to tap into their energies.

Working with Planet Transits and Aspects

The last aspect of time we work with is to connect with the planets as they transit and aspect our natal chart. This is by far the most powerful form of timing I have worked with.

A good website for determining the planetary hours according to the second planetary hour system is: http://www.astrology.com.tr/planetary-hours.asp

A good website for transits to birth charts: https://alabe.com/freechart/Daily.asp

The chapter with my ritual experiences shares a little bit of the work and insights I gained while working with my planetary transits.

Sigils

Spirit sigils/signatures are seals or keys from which we open the spirit's domain with. They are particular geometric patterns connected with a specific energetic formation. By opening these doors we touch in with the spirit's domain and the intelligences and energies therein.

Acquiring Materials

While acquiring tools, stones, and other objects is something an adept does over time, I feel it is important to at the very least acquire the metals rather than using paper for the spirit's sigil. You can get copper, steel, aluminum, and tin sheets at most hardware stores and some craft stores. As for lead, I always get fishing weights and melt them outdoors. As they melt you will see a shinny silvery substance and some bland grey chunky stuff. Decant the liquid silvery substance on wax paper and allow it to harden – that's the lead. As for silver, I purchased my metal disks in Santa Fe many years ago. I do not have gold so I went to a bison farm and purchased some skin to make my sigil with.

If for some reason you are not able to acquire the metals you can always draw them on the tree bark that corresponds with the planet. If that is not an option, then you can make your own paper, infusing it with herbs and whatever else relates with the planet you are working with.

To make paper: save some paper from bills or whatever and shred it. Then place the shredded pieces of paper in a bucket of water and allow it to soak for at least a few days – if you can do this while the planet you are working with is visible and aspected well, then set the bucket outside to capture the light. You can infuse the water with herbs, minerals, oils, et cetera.

After the paper has soaked for a couple of days, place it in a blender and turn it into paste. Pour the paste onto a screen (window screen works well), add in whatever herbs, stones, or stuff you wish, smooth the pulp down and set it in an airy place to dry. Once it is dry you can peel it off the screen, sand it down a little, cut it to the shape you want, and use it to make your sigils.

When to Create Sigil

The Arbatel suggests we create the sigil during the morning hour of the planet we are working with and then later commence with the ritual. I did this with ARATRON's and OCH's sigils, only later did I personally find it more beneficial to do it during the beginning of my night ritual. In other words, during my evening rituals I would inscribed the sigils while inviting the Olympic energies into my circle. I found this helpful towards building a relationship with them directly.

If you wish to optimize your energetic connection with the planet, so as to make it the most conducive to invite the spirit's energy, you can consider the planetary alignments, aspects, lunar and solar cycles, as well as, day and time. Otherwise, just make it simple and make a connection however you wish.

Inscribing

Draw, paint, inscribe, or carve the sigils with full awareness and intention. If you find yourself thinking, are moody, emotionally upset, dwelling, foggy, anxious, or in any other unbalanced state:

stop. It is better to inscribe the sigil on the wrong day and hour than to be mentally, emotionally, physically or energetically unbalanced on the perfect day and time.

When you inscribe the sigil make sure to have it embedded within the mind. This is the key to sigils. To invite and work with the energetic and spiritual spheres it's best to align the physical and mental planes while creating the sigils.

As you inscribe the sigil, surround yourself with those energies you are seeking to invite. If it is HAGITH's sigil, then surround yourself with vernal energies, drink some hibiscus or some other tea akin to her energy, listen to corresponding music and so on. Bring all that energy into the sigil while intoning HAGITH's name. Vibrate her energy and channel it into the sigil's substance.

When inscribing or drawing the sigil it is important to align all your energy (thoughts and feelings) upon it, for we are not only physically drawing out the sigil, the key, we are actually opening the door within our minds. So we visualize it, we imprint it upon our minds, we embody its energy.

Initially the physical sigil is a means to invite and hold the energy within our circle. It is literally a key that opens the energetic plane for the spirit to enter from. After infusing the energy within us, the actual sigil, like all our tools, are no longer needed. But in the beginning, it is quite helpful in my experience.

When we draw the energy upon the paper
skin
metal
stone
bark
or what have you,
visualize it within the mind and vibrate the spirit's name –
calling it forth:
set the frame/plane from which the energy can arise and abide within your circle –
your life.

That's how we invite the energy.
The sigil is the key that opens the pathway/door for the energy to flow through.

Below is an example of what I say while inscribing the sigil:

Vibrating PH-uuuuuu-llllll

We inscribe your sigil –
your key upon this silver,
building a connection –
a Pathway 4 2 to B-come 1.

Infuse this metal with your energy and essence.
Bless us with your wisdom and intelligence.

Thank You
Thank You
Thank You

PH-uuuuuuu-lllllll

Grounding

As we enter into the planetary sphere the sigil becomes the key we use to invite those energies we seek. It is also helpful in anchoring our consciousness least we get lost within those realms we are investigating.

When you find your mind wandering,
hold the sigil in your Hand,
seek the ground from within the plane you are working with by burning incense,
visualizing the sigil,
and intoning/invoking the spirit's name.

****

I don't know about you, but I do not have complete control over my mind, yet. Every once in a while during ritual I find my mind veering away, getting lost. So, Bethor showed me how to realign my focus with the energy by placing harmonious herbs on the coal and restating my intention for the ritual. It's amazing how the mind and energy instantly shifts to our desired ends: not only that, but there is a surplus of energy and clarity that comes with it.

Deciphering

To decipher a sigil we need to know its parts and their relationship to one another, as well as, with the whole in general. When considering the parts one thing to meditate on is its physical characteristics. Shape being one of those. Each shape, be it a letter, directionality, size, rigid/smooth, closed/open, high/low, surfaces, angles, points, and so forth, all embody a particular energy.

An Adept utilizes those energies to create/encompass/radiate/give form to a particular energy. In the same way, a spirit's sigil has a particular energy vibration, and it's name and key (sigil) help us to tap into and understand that energy, intelligence and wisdom.

Another facet of deciphering a sigil is to look at it as a Rochester inkblot: what images and thoughts come to mind when you look at the symbol. For instance, when I looked at ARATRON's sigil, the following image came up:

Like a bridge crossing the stream,
the earth giving radiant energy from its core,
flowing,
springing up from the earth:
ARATRON offers a bridge to the other side.

This is the image I saw while meditating on ARATRON's sigil. The earth is the encompassing three lines that are open to the heavens (rectangle three dimensions), and inside the open rectangle there is a rigid shape like a volcano/spring coming up from the earth's surface, and over that is a bridge we can connect the sides 2-gether with.

Working with Sigils

There are many ways to work with a sigil. Beyond using it as a key to open the spirit's energies into our circle and lives, we can use it to transfer the planetary energies onto other things. For instance, before I smoke Herb in a ritual I will place it upon the sigil so that the spirit's energy may be infused within the Herb. By touching any object with the sigil, the sigil's energies will infuse within that object.

Another way of absorbing the energy is to reflect the candles light from the metal's surface upon objects or beings. As the light reflects off the surface it absorbs the energy and transfers it to whatever thing it touches. For instance, reflecting the candle's light off the sigil's surface upon ourselves (image on next page).

To invite the light into yourself, you reflect the candles light off of the sigil's surface upon your face, then look into that light fully so that it may enter into your being and begin to react with your energy.

First do it with both eyes,
then close one and take in the light through the other,
then switch,
now open both eyes again and receive:
We invite your energies in,
we call upon you [Spirit's Name],
vibrating your name,
receiving your light,
we open to your energy and embody your essence.

Feel the energy shifting your energetic matrix.

Once we have imbued ourselves with the planetary energy we can bring the sigil to our Third-eye and use the back of its surface to reflect the candle's light down upon the altar.

We no longer need to reflect the light upon ourselves,
for we are those energies, forces, and so on.

And so,
with the sigil facing out,
we reflect the light off of the its surface,
sending our Will and Intention out into the Universe.

The difference now is,

we are directing the light/energy as it emanates from within us.
We reflect the altars light down upon the altar like a spot light,
and whatever the light shines upon will be activated by the energy.
****

Hold the metal up and look at the Spirit's sigil. Now, turning it around, angle the sigil a little until the candle's light reflects off the metal's surface and shines down on the altar. Like a spot light, you can shine the light upon whatever surface, object, thing you wish to. You are, in a very real since, sending this particular energy you have inscribe on the metal into whatever thing you wish.

Parting

Unlike elementals, demons, and even angelic beings, the Olympic Spirits are less likely to mess with our energies when we are out of the circle. In saying, I do not find it necessary to do a full fledge banishing ritual to send the spirits away. In fact, I found it more beneficial to just give thanks and a parting good-bye, much like I do with a friend.

Below is an example of what I do at the end of my Olympic Rituals:

Holding the sigil over the coals
I burn some pine sap that I harvested from Arizona.

Vibrating ARATRON's name,
Giving thanks,
I request what I seek from him,
then, giving thanks again, I vibrate ARATRON's name while wrapping his sigil in black silk. Then visualizing the sigil in my mind, I blow out the candle, and as the smoke dissipates, so does the sigil within my mind's eye.

Nothing spectacular, but quite effective in dissipating the energy.

Intentions

One thing I do in ritual, is to charge my ritual items in such a way as to bless whoever touches them. For instance, when I charge the sigils I have the following in mind:

May good energies and essences be imbued within this metal,
and may whoever possesses and knows of its virtues
and who calls upon its virtues with a clear mind and pure heart
receive its blessings and be completely fulfilled.

I am about positivity, growth, abundance, compassion, and all that good stuff. While there are times for getting dirty and fighting, it is a mistake to abide at that level of being when we do not have to.

In saying, when we commune with a friend or with any energy for that matter, it is my opinion that we should do so in such a way as to invite joy, health, abundance, and goodness rather than sickness, disease, hatred, anger, fear, distrust, need, and so forth.

By keeping our intentions and motivations pure, we minimize the negativity in our lives while attracting the positive. And I don't know about you, but that's what I want in my life.

Mantras

Unlike calling someone's name, working with a spirit's name is more like a mantra: we intone their names. While I could give hard and fast rules on how to vibrate a spirit's name, I personally suggest you play around with the name yourself and find out what works for you.

The key is to find the right vibratory frequency to activate the spirit's energy into your life. We are all different, and so, while vibrations will have a similar effect/affect upon us, no two experiences will ever be the same.

For instance, when working with HAGITH I have found a few different ways to work with her energy.

HAGITH

Placing her herbs on the coal,
visualize HAGITH's sigil in my mind's eye:

Haaaaaa-g-iiiii-thhhhh

Bringing the energy up,
extending the "th" sound into silence.
Feel the energy.

****

Holding her sigil in my hand,
with eyes closed,
I vibrated HAGITH's name.
Feel the Ha vibration in your lower region,

feel it stimulate and get things moving.
Then with the G,
shift and stabilize the energy in the gut before vibrating the iiiiiii in the heart and then extending and spreading the energy out with the "Th."

I notice the energy comes into my mouth and then slowly disperses throughout my head as the thhhhhhh moves into silence.

Arms up,
encircled with your energy vibrating within me.

First emphasizing the Ha
by its volume and length
Haaaaaaaaaagiiithh

Then bring the energy up –
focus and vibrate haaagiiiiithhhhh

Now focus on the lips
lengthen the thhhhhhh into silence

Be at peace.

****

The above intonation was my way of ending the ritual. I opened my arms and hugged myself before vibrating her name.

ARATRON

While HAGITH's name invited the feeling of energy rising and vibrating within me, intoning ARATRON felt like the energy sunk into me.

ARrrrr-Ahh-Troooooonnnnnn

Sometimes just saying ARATRON's name was enough to solidify his energy in my sphere.

According to Eastern Traditions there are three levels of mantra work: audible, whisper, and mental – mental being the most powerful. When working with external forces and bodily energies I have found intoning the spirit's name audibly to be the most effective. When working on stabilizing and focusing the mind I have found mental intonation to be the most effective. As for whispering, I found it to be a mix of the two.

Beyond inviting a spirit's energy into our life and stabilizing our minds, mantras are useful in sending, spreading and solidifying energy, and in attracting, condensing and breaking down energy as well.

Coupling a spirit's sigil with the intonation of their name in a conducive environment while having a focused mind is a great way to invite their energies into our lives. I see the sigil as a key to open their planes, the intonation of their name as a way of calling and creating a vibratory bridge from which they can enter into our circle with, and the incense, stones and other corresponding energies become a means for them to work within our sphere.

Holding the sigil over the coals,
I burn the pine sap that I harvested from Arizona.

Vibrating ARATRON name.
Thanking.
Requesting my intentions.
Giving thanks.
Vibrating ARATRON's name again,
I wrap his sigil in black silk.
Visualize his sigil,
I blow out the candle,
and as the smoke dissipates,
so does the sigil from my mind's eye.

OCH

OCH's mantra can be intoned in many ways,
the newest way I have learned is

OOOOOOOOO-CH! A very sharp ending or OOOOOOOOOO-Chhhhhhh… a long drawn out one.

When we work with mantras it reformulates our bodily energies. Some claim that mantras can in fact crystallize our body structures, making them impenetrable to external forces and energies. I have not personally found that to be true, but I can say I have worked with mantras to get rid of negativity from my life, sped up healing, dissipated negative thinking patterns (larvas and phantoms) and opened different energy levels in my body/mind.

When we intone a spirit's name we are vibrating their essence within us. To me that is one of the most powerful aspects of working with mantras. We are literally inviting the spirit's energy into our lives. Part of Theurgia is the embodiment of an entity's energy. We are Gods, all of us. The more energies we connect with, the more powerful and wise we become. A Great Adept has at the very least worked with and mastered the bodily, elemental and celestial energies.

PHUL

Phe-yul

PH- ULLLLL

PH – teeth on lower lip then make a strong "F" sound while opening the mouth and releasing the lower lip.

ULlllll- start with the energy opening the whole torso then sinking the energy with the "L" sound, slowly deepening the sound of the vibration until, in silence, the energy brings you down to the lower parts of your being.

Rest there.

Feel the energy.

****

There are many different ways to categorize the magical traditions. One way is to consider Low and High Magic. While this designation is a little outdated, there is some validity to defining magic in this way.

Traditionally there are a few different ways to look at Low and High Magic. The first way is to see Low Magic as working only with the Lunar and Elemental Planes while High Magic adds in working with the Celestial and other Planes.

A second way I have heard this demarcation justified is that Low Magic is all about causing external change while High Magic adds in internal change.

However we parse it, the Arbatel is definitely focused on the High Magical Traditions. It not only seeks to effect physical change, but internal as well. The point is to develop ourselves by processing through and mastering all dimensions of our beings.

When working with PHUL's name I found myself becoming more aware of my mouth and the way sounds emanate from me. Awareness is one of the gifts mantras give us. For they are not only sound waves, physical motions, mental activities and emotional movements, they are also energetic patterns that resonant with particular universal forces.

They bring us into ourselves and then act as a means to send out sound, vision and energy.

It is very important to visualize the spirit's sigil while opening the body/mind to the spirit's energy. If we just say the name without the visualization, it just muddles the thoughts and energy, and sometimes even invites unbalance.

PHALEG

PH-Ahhh-Laaaaaay-G

The "F" sound is carried
like an echo
through all three states of being:
unconscious
conscious
Superconscious,
then the A,
that alchemical symbol of fire forming the triangle,
and then LEG,
a line and downward movement as if stepping down the volume while we enter into silence with G.

There is power in mantras. As we vibrate the name we send out our intentions, will, visions and energy. It is also used to transform energies. I have experienced firsthand how mantras convert negative energies into positive ones and vice versa. I have used mantras to shift my mind and shift the environment.

Just recently I witness two people get into a fight with a bunch of other kids standing around instigating them. As I watched the fight unfold I found myself working with overtones and my heart chakra. I sent out love and peace. Within a few moments the fight dissolved and everyone went their separate ways.

Did it have anything to do with my efforts? Absolutely.

Every letter, every sound has power and meaning. Be this inherent within the symbol and sound or contrived and adopted by the Adept is often debated. To me, it does not matter. What matters is the effect, and I can assure you, there is definitely an effect and an affect.

When you intone a spirit's name you can actually feel the vibrations working on a cellular level.

Some mantras sooth and calm the body's energy while others excite and aggravate it. Keeping this in mind, when we work with a spirit's name, we intone it according to their nature.

For PHALEG that means with power, intensity and strength. Visualize yourself as a powerful force vibrating the name: PHA-LEEEG. Emphasis the PHA and G when intoning. Feel the power rise up in you. Become the energy.

Everything is vibrating. Learning to touch in, absorb and radiate it; that's the key towards effectively influencing the world around and within you. Great Adepts like Agrippa, Dee, and Pythagoras are just a few who have utilized the power of sound to understand and work with the energies of life.

One thing I learned from PHALEG was to use intonations as a means to invite more energy into my life. He reminded me of a story I heard about some French Benedictine's who stopped chanting for a time. During that time they started to become more sluggish and in need of more sleep. Their health declined and their state of minds became foggy and listless. When chanting was resumed they regained their health and mental clarity, and once again only needed a few hours of sleep.

Another aspect of working with PHALEG's name was to invite strength and courage. When I am feeling lethargic I intone PHALEG's name to wake up. Also, when I am feeling overwhelmed, being attacked, or in the mist of arguing with others, I have found intoning PHALEG's name helps me shore up my energy and give me more vitality and strength to work and deal with conflict in my life.

If we can see and understand Life as energy, then it is not difficult to see how and why mantras are so effective.

OPHIEL

OOO-PHeeee-EEELLL

Mantras are vibratory energy patterns that work on all levels of being. As we vibrate the sound within our being, within our minds, we can experience it vibrating out into the Universe: literally. This in turn helps us tap into different intelligences and energies throughout the Universe.

There are many parts to a mantra

1. There is a spirit, energy, intelligence, deity, and so forth connected with the sound
2. There is a tone, inflection, volume, meter, sound and texture
3. Emotions, thoughts, and conscious experiences
4. Specific energy and force
5. Forms (sigils) and manifestations

Part of what OPHIEL has taught me is the utilization of mantras to touch in with different intellectual spheres. While we intone the spirit's name, we are opening its plane of being within us. Once the plane is open to us, we can begin to question the spirit and investigate its sphere of influence.

Some guidelines to follow when intoning a Spirit's name

1. Calm and clear the mind of all distractions
2. Focus
3. Intentional
4. Reverential
5. Learn as much as you can about the spirit you are invoking
6. Smooth, regular intoning
7. Work in sync with the breath
8. Visualize sigil being activated by the name (becoming brighter, shifting colors, etc.)
9. Incorporate the use of colors, lighting, incense, hand gestures, body postures, and whatever other tool that will further empower and strengthen your efforts.
10. Infuse yourself with the energy and radiate it

BETHOR

BEEEE (e sounds like pet)-THOOORRRRRR

Two things BETHOR has taught me are to extend my energy field out and to open to higher frequencies of Being.

Intoning a spirit's name aligns are energy fields with theirs. It is important to find our ground after working with different energies. This is something ARATRON taught me, but only after having frazzled myself while working with BETHOR.

When we extend ourselves too far or jump into the deep end before learning how to swim, we can really screw ourselves up. It is the same with working with spirits. Be aware of that.

Incense

Incense is a great way to connect with the spirits. By combining specific herbs, trees and minerals, we are able to invite their specific energies into our sphere. By inhaling the smoke, we bring that energy into our being – absorbing it. Then, as we exhale, we send out our energy in order to manifest our intentions.

It is important to visualize this exchange. When we inhale, we see the spirit's energy being imbued within us. Allow it to saturate every cell, every particle of your being. Then, as you exhale, attach your prayers, thoughts, energy to the smoke, and visualize it filling your circle and extending to the four corners of the Universe.

One thing I have found helpful in absorbing the energy is to bring the smoke all around me with my hands. Literally grabbing the smoke and surrounding my body/mind with it. Then, with full awareness, I inhale – taking it in.

As for what ingredients to use, that is up to you. Research the internet, different books, and whatever else you can get your hands on, and find what works for you. Also, be aware of the herbs, for some are poisonous and can really harm you.

A couple things to consider is the mixture. Does one ingredient dominate the mixture, and if so, how can you balance it in such a way that each herb can be distinguished when burning the mix. It is important to find a balance with the herbs. This not only insures that the subtle energies can all be worked with, but it also insures that we can work with the energies in a balanced way: internally and externally.

One way to do this is to add each ingredient individually. Start with the denser herbs, as they take longer to burn, then progressively add the rest of the ingredients in this order: roots, bark, fruits, resins, leaves and flowers.

As to when we burn the incense, I use to have the coal burning incense constantly. The problem with this is that sometimes the coal gets smothered. We can prevent this by grounding the ingredients into a find powder and only adding a little bit at a time.

Personally, I add incense to the coal, infuse myself with the energy, and then commune with the energies and intelligences I called forth by fully absorbing myself in the spirit's sphere. I sometimes go thirty minutes or so before I find the energy wavering. Only then do I add more incense to the coal. This stabilizes the energy and helps bring me back into the spirit's sphere.

One benefit of mixing the herbs together instead of placing them individually on the coal is that each pinch will exhibit its own energetic flavor. This in turn helps us connect with the energies in different ways. Experiment and find out for yourself.

As for which coals I have found to be the best, Three Kings Incense Hookah Coals and Swift Lite charcoals burn consistently for about an hour.

When burning a group of things one after the other,
do it first with the densest:
roots
bark
fruits,
and then,
as it smolders,
add the resins, leaves and flowers.

Inhale my essence,
pull me in,
absorb my energy,
embody my power.

Bring the smoke in –
my energy,
encircle yourself,
be absorbed within.

Don't lose focus:
direct the energy to where you want it to go.

We offer our gifts (incense)
and then our prayers.

We seek love
compassion
and balance between body, emotions and mind.

We seek pleasures
enjoyment
beauty
and joy.

These gifts of yours we seek,
please hear our call.

May these herbs (rose and lemon verbena)
be pleasing to you HAGITH:
Enjoy.

We have opened this space to you,
honoring you and your energy.

Please come,
we welcome you into our lives.

Placing the herbs on the coal.
I offer you these herbs great ARATRON.

My essence
energy
mind
being
prayers
intentions:
this is who I am

Hear my call,
I call unto you.

My Planetary Mix

Moon: willow and sensimilla
Mercury: lavender and gum Arabic
Venus: rose and passion flower
Sun: cinnamon and amber
Mars: blood root and pepper (use multi-colored that you have ground yourself)
Jupiter: cedar and oak
Saturn: pine and myrrh

It is not about keeping the censor smoking,
but about offering our gifts,
taking in the essence,
and infusing ourselves within the planetary sphere.

When we find ourselves being drawn out of the sphere,
we again offer our incense and go back in.

When working with the incense, a good mix is one where each of the energies are distinguished, in other words, we are able to distinguish each smell individually and as a whole.

Bring the smoke in first with the right hand,
then the left,
now with both hands;
encircle yourself within the smoke,
bring it in,
In-hail and Be Filled:
B Fulfilled

Each pinch of incense is unique.

Sometime the solar energy is stronger,
other times all I can feel is Mars pushing through.
Saturn is pungent while Venus is lovely and enjoyable.

Feel the difference,
see where the thoughts go,
what is happening?

The cool thing about integrating energies together through incense mixes is that, whenever you find yourself burning that mix, that energy will be awoken within you, eliciting a similar experience.

Working with BETHOR and PHALEG

I really like Frankincense and Pewen sap combined;
not so much Frankincense and Dragon's Blood.

****

One way of combining two energies is to mix their herbs in such a way that it agrees with our tastes while at the same time combining different aspects of the planetary energies together in order to gain understanding and control over them.

So, in the above case, both dragon's blood and pewen are martial energies, and yet, dragon's blood and frankincense did not resonant with me while pewen and frankincense did: I actually liked it.

This is a simple way of beginning to learn how to combined different energies 2-gether. I like dragon's blood, it is very martial, but I am not looking for the raw draconian energies, but the refined, wise energies of Mars that are in alignment with the higher states of mind I seek, all the while of course, grounding into the earth and centering within the heart. That Mars energy is what I seek to embody.

Rituals

For those expecting complex invocations and prayers, an eclectic assortment of tools and supplies, large and intricate circles, body postures, certain tones and inflections of voice, and a host of other insane ritualistic etiquette, this is not the grimoire for you.

In fact, out of all the grimoires I have been honored to study and work with, this is the most simple and down to earth that I have come across.

The following is my ritual process as I imagine the Tree of Life in-folding:

1. First I clear up the space and set it up (Malkut)
2. Then I clear away all the subconscious and unconscious baggage least it arises and interferes with my ritual (Yesod)
3. I do the calls and invite the spirit's intelligence (Hod)
4. Touching in with the spirit, I seek to commune and work with its energies (Netzach)
5. Inviting the spirit's beneficial energies into my consciousness and being, while getting rid of the unwanted energies (Tiphareth).
6. Transforming and transmuting the energies to my intentions (Geburah)
7. Extending the energies (Chesed)
8. Solidifying the energies and bringing about physical manifestation (Binah)
9. Reconfiguring the spirit's energies and making it part of my energetic matrix (Chokmah)
10. Theurgia (Kether)

Prior to every ritual I study the spirit's domain, energies, intellectual realms and conscious states. Then I clear up my ritual area, turn off all electronic distractions/interruptions, smudge the area, tools and self, and then sit down to clear my mind, finding my ground and center before focusing upon the ritual's intention. At this point I allow whatever thoughts or energies to arise within my mind in order to resolve them so that my ritual can commence without internal or external interruptions.

After settling the mind and body, I light the candle and call upon my teachers, guides, and protectors to be with me. I light the candle knowing that it is a Divine Spark of Life. By holding this understanding and visualization in my mind, I am literally inviting the highest understanding I have of the Divine into my ritual and life.

Having set the energies, I smoke some Herb. Inhaling, I take in the planetary energies, and then, as I exhale, I state my intention for the ritual. After a few tokes, I place some planetary herbs on the incense coal, hold the spirit's sigil over the smoke, visualize the sigil in my mind, while invoking the spirit to come forth to bless us with its energy and essence – guiding, strengthening and supporting us in our endeavors.

During the first few moments I just sit with the energy, feeling the spirit as it comes into the circle and into my space.

Then I ask questions and listen to the responses.

After questioning, I seek to solidify and amplify the spirit's positive energies in my life while dissolving and banishing those qualities and energies of the spirit that I do not wish to have in my life.

Through that process I slowly absorb the spirit's energies and intelligences. This leads to the embodiment of the spirit's essence. No longer is the spirit necessary, for the Adept has integrated the spirit's intelligence and energy into his or her B-ing. It is a long process filled with many ups and downs. So don't get discourage.

It is a very simple ritual. The only tools I use are a candle and totemic, mineral, metallic, and herbal substances that correspond with the energies I am working with. It's very beneficial to have at least one item from each of the four compounded bodies that resonate with the spirit's energy: metals, stones, animals and plants. Even so, it is not necessary as long as you have the sigil and name of the spirit you're working with.

Once you've commenced the ritual and have called forth the energy I suggest you just sit for a moment and feel.

Does anything come up?

Is there a block or some issue preventing you from connecting with the spirit?
Is the mind muddled,
frazzled,
cloudy,
on overdrive?

How about the energy,
is it stagnant
twisted
blocked
clogged?

Process through these things and move on.

A point is reached when the mind rests:
living
knowing
understanding –
rest within that state and you will find yourself connecting with the spirit and its energy.

To help prepare you for ritual, make an effort to study and learn about the energy/energies you are going to work with. Don't just go into ritual blind and ignorant.

Once you have a basic understanding of the energies, consider what you want to accomplish and then gather those things that will support your undertaking.

Take into consideration those objects and things you already possess that resonant with the energies you are calling forth. For instance, when I was learning about Saturn I found that I already connected with two particular energies of that sphere: Willow and Pine.

By utilizing these in ritual I was already familiar with some of Saturn's energies, and so, was able to connect with ARATRON a lot quicker than if I had nothing in common with his energy and essence.

*As a side note, I tried working with the invocations the Arbatel offered, but due to my Solomonic days, I have become disenchanted with long, drawn out invocations and prayers that cause more trouble than they are worth. I have found, even with the Solomonic works, that simple, truthful, and to the point invocations are a lot more effective – especially when they are personalized to our own temperament, style and intention.

Spirits

While there are many different ways/levels/approaches/perspectives/et cetera to work with energies and intelligences, I have found there to be three general stages:

First we learn about and experience their energies and combinations:

What thoughts and emotions arise?
What happens to our environment after touching in with their energies?
What is different – if anything?
What memories arise?
What kinds of things are showing up in our life?
Who do we find ourselves connecting with/attracted to or repulsed from?
Who is popping up in our life?
How is our overall mood?

Paying attention to these and other such things help us gain a deeper understanding of the forces we are working with.

The second stage is all about utilizing those energies to accomplish our aims. This is also when we start to directly communicate with the intelligences of each sphere/plane, learning about the mysteries of ourselves and the world around us. During this phase we learn about those things we can do to accomplish our aims. Let me say that again: "What we can do." Too many practitioners believe that all they have to do is wave their wands and the world will bow at their feet. For me, more so than anything else, it is about listening to what we are taught and applying those things in our lives.

The last stage arises when we understand their motions and the effects they have in the world and the affects they have in our lives. Unlike the first stage where we are just learning about these energies, in this stage we know. There is no ambiguity or uncertainty: for we are those energies.

This is also when we begin to work with the planetary transits to deepen our understandings, widen our knowledge, and extend our wisdom to include all facets of our beings/manifestations, as well as, all other areas of interest to us☺

Now, to the million dollar question: "Are Spirits Real?"

It all depends on how you look at things.

Are there disembodied energies out there that likely have some intelligence that contain information, movement, and so forth? Yes.

Are they sentient?

One thing is for certain,
when I touch in with those energies there is definitely dialog,
exchange,
expansion and growth.

Is it just psychological processes going on inside there,
or are there real external forces that can and do interact and influence us?

I guess one question we could ask that might shine light upon this issue is, "What relationship does energy, consciousness and matter have to do with each other, and why is space-time so important to their interactions?"

It's not an easy question to answer, nor in truth, might there ever really be a satisfying answer. For there's no scientific instrument that can definitively give us the answer. If there was, there would not be so many vying beliefs regarding spirits. There's just too much unknown to really ever know. But, as some adepts have come to appreciate, it's not so much about external validation of a spirit's existence but the process and affect/effect that arises when we work with them.

I personally choose to opt out of the debate all together and instead just look at everything as energy. At that level there is a lot less contention. For harmful energy, no matter the name, will affect us in certain ways just as nourishing energy will. Choosing what energy is best suited for our purposes makes sense to me. And giving it a name so that we can relate to, and tap into it, is good as well.

While I do not offer a definitive answer to this ongoing question, I can offer this: when we invoke these energies into our lives they trigger physical, environmental, financial, emotional, social, mental, energetic, and spiritual movements in our lives. If spirits are just psychological processes as some claim, than how is it that these energies and forces affect/effect so much more than just the mental and emotional planes?

PLANTARY CORREPONDENCES

Jupiter	37
Venus	40
Saturn	42
Sun	45
Moon	47
Mars	50
Mercury ..	52

These correspondences arise from many different sources and traditions. A few of the more pertinent sources are listed in the reference section. Those things bolded are what I have worked with in that planetary sphere directly and can attest to. Some correspondences I disagree with, but for completions sake, I have recorded most everything I have come across. It is up to you to find out what works for you.

Jupiter

Metal: **Tin**

Signs: Sagittarius and Pisces

Day: Thursday

Sephirot: Chesed (Kindness, Mercy)

Golden Dawn Grade: Adeptus Exemptus

Elements: Air and Water

State: Warm and Moist

Humor: Sanguine

Root Number: Four

Symbols: Thunderbolt, **wand**, **crystal ball**, scepter, throne

Tarot: Wheel of Fortune

Day: 9 hours and 56 earth minutes

Year: About 12 earth years

Olympic Spirit: BETHOR

Heptarchical King: Ynepor

King of Jinn: Shem huresh (The Name Huresh)

Archangel: Zadkiel/Sachiel

Angelical Order: Dominions/Chashmalim

Planetary Angel: Tzadqiel

Planetary Intelligence: Jophiel

Planetary Spirit: Hismael

Dieties: Zeus, Marduk, Tinia, Taranis

Stones: **Amethyst**, **lapis lazuli**, sapphire, diamond, topaz

Taste: Salty

Plants: Agrimony, aloe, amaranth, artichoke, barberry, barley, bearberry, bell pepper, borage, betony, bladderwrack and other seaweeds for saltiness, blessed thistle, blue cohosh, borage, butcher's broom, carrot, celery, chaparral, chervil, chicory, clover, ginseng, cinquefoil, clover, comfrey, thyme, echinacea, couch grass, crampbark, curly dock, dandelion, dock, dogbane, **mistletoe**, pennyroyal, **eyebright**, fennel, **fenugreek**, feverfew, **fig**, flax, ginger, goldenseal, grapefruit, horsetail, hops, **hyssop**, Irish moss, lady's slipper, licorice, linden flower, lobelia, **marjoram**, marshmallow, milk thistle, mint, mullein, pumpkin seed, **sunflower**, **saffron**, **sage**, skullcap, stevia, wheat, yarrow

Trees: Ash, balm, **birch**, brazil nut, chestnut, cascara, **cedar**, elm, hawthorn, grapefruit, **juniper**, magnolia, **maple**, **fir**, nutmeg, **oak**, **olive**, **pau d'arco**, pear, poplar, **sarsaparilla**, **slippery elm**, **sweet gum**, tulip tree, **walnut**, **white willow**

Colors: Blues and some Purples

Birds: **Eagle**, cuckoo, lark, **peacock**

Animals: **Horse**, ox, **stag**, **elk**, sheep
Water Animals: Dolphins,

Mystical Beings: **Centaurs**, unicorns, incubi

Body: Liver, digestion, metabolism, hips, thighs, legs, feet, arteries

Mystical Virtue: Sublimation

Vice: Gluttony

Antidote to vice: Temperance

Areas of Influence: Politics, religion, faith, law, extension, enlargement, expansion, increase, gambling, speculations, travel, gains, riches, favors, honors, dignities, luck, protection, prosperity, success in endeavors, honors, robust health

General Qualities/Characteristics: Nobility, forthrightness, altruistic, high-minded, aligned with High Ideals, merging with something larger, greater understanding, philosophical and religious tolerance and expression, open-minded, inspired, faithful, taking a chance, rising above pettiness, prophesy, supportive, uplifting, buoyancy, spacious, universalizing, understanding, abstract, unitive, honorable, just, trustworthy,

Negative Qualities/Characteristics: Self-righteous, intolerance, greedy, cultish, excessive, distant, tactless, over-extending, over look details, lofty, self-deceiving, uncompromising, egotistical, careless, pretentious, exaggeration, rash, gullible, boasting, lazy, ungrounded, pompous, bigot, hypocrite

Venus

Metal: **Copper**

Signs: Taurus and Libra

Day: Friday

Sephirot: Netzach (Victory)

Golden Dawn Grade: Philosophus

Elements: Earth, Water and Air

State: Warm and Moist

Humor: Phlegmatic

Root Number: 7

Symbols: **Mirror**, jewelry, **perfume**, hair, girdle, **seashells**

Tarot: Empress

Day: 243 earth days

Year: 225 earth days

Olympic Spirit: HAGITH

Heptarchical King: Aligon

King of Jinn: Zawba'ah (The Storm)

Archangel: Haniel/Anael

Angelical Order: Principalities/Elohim

Planetary Angel: Haniel/Usiel

Planetary Intelligence: Hagiel/Kedemel

Planetary Spirit: Beni Elohim

Deities: Aphrodite, Venus, Ishtar, Lakshmi, Bast

Taste: Sweet

Stones: **Emerald**, **rose quartz**, turquoise, **opal**, **jade**, loadstone, chrysolite, coral

Plants: Ambrosia, **angelica**, apples, artichoke, **baby's breath**, beans, berries, birthwort, bitter melon, blackberry, **bleeding hearts**, broccoli, bugleweed, burdock, cabbage, cardamom, **catnip**, celery, chickpea, cinquefoil, clover, coltsfoot, columbine, cucumber, daffodil, daisy, damiana, **fern**, feverfew, fig, figwort, flax, forget-me-not, fuchsia, geranium, goldenrod, gooseberry, **hibiscus**, **heartsease**, hollyhock, honeysuckle, **jasmine**, jewelweed, jimsonweed, **kava-kava**, kindneywort, lady's bedstraw, lady's mantle, lamb's ear, larkspur, lemon balm, **lemon verbena**, lily, lily of the valley, lovage, mallow, **meadowsweet**, moneywort, monkshood, mugwort, **passion flower and fruit**, periwinkle, pinks, plantain, **primrose**, pumpkin, ragword, **raspberry**, **rose**, **rosehips**, rose mallow, **self-heal**, sesame, silverweed, soapwort, sorrel, spearmint, **strawberry**, sweet breath, tansy, thyme, valerian, Venus flytrap, **verbena**, **vervain**, **violet**, yarrow

Trees: **Almond**, **apple**, apricot, **avocado**, **banana**, **birch**, cashew, **cherry**, crabapple, elder, **eucalyptus**, heather, **lemon**, **myrtle**, olive, pear, plum, **pomegranate**, sweet gum, sycamore, **willow**

Colors: Greens and pinks

Birds: Sparrow, **dove**, **swan**, partridge, nightingale, pheasant

Animals: **Rabbit**, **bull**, calves, civet cat, panther, sheep

Water Animals: Dolphins, **tortoise**, **crab**, pilchards, gilthead, whiting

Insects, arachnids, reptiles, and others: Butterflies, lady bugs

Mystical Beings: Succubi, gorgons, **faeries**, harpies, fauns, mermaids, sirens

Body: Kidneys, urinary system, sexual organs, skin, hormones, bladder, uterus, ovaries, testes, prostate, tongue, emotions, shoulders, arms

Mystical Virtues: Integration and Enjoyment
Vice: Lust

Antidotes to vice: Self-control, Redirection and Gratitude

Areas of Influence: Love, healing, garden, pleasures, harmony, joy, arts, beauty, sensuality, relaxation, luxury, money, emotions, emotional healing, prosperity, desire, fertility, feminine persuasion, enticement, seduction, assimilation, good fortune, relationships, kindness

General Characteristics: Sensual, magnetic, expressive, artistic, laid back, kind, loving, nurturing, easy going, friendly, social, fun, visionary, glamorous, imaginative, connected with body, graceful, likeable, charming, peacemaker, idealistic, passionate, receptive, empathic, witty, soft, gentle, poetic expression

Negative Qualities: Foggy, avoidance, dramatic, emotionally isolated or over the top, obsessive, compulsive, addictive, dreamer/fantasizing, superficial, plastic, attachments, two-faced, resentful, sentimental, jealous, self-centered, vampiristic, demanding, flowery, possessive, needy, moody, insecure, nagging, criticizing, complacent, lazy, over-indulgent, fickle, manipulator, distractible, irritable

Saturn

Metals: **Lead** and pewter

Signs: Capricorn and Aquarius

Day: Saturday

Sephirot: Binah (Understanding)

Golden Dawn Grade: Magister Templi

Element: Earth

State: Cold and Dry

Humor: Melancholic

Root Number: 3

Symbols: Scythe, keys, altar, hourglass, **cauldron, cloak**

Tarot: Death and World

Day: 10 earth hours 39 minutes

Year: 29 earth years

Olympic Spirit: ARATRON

Heptarchical King: Napsen

King of Jinn: Maymon (Prosperous)

Archangel: Zaphkiel/Cassiel

Angelical Order: Thrones/Aralim

Planetary Angel: Kassiel/Kerubiel

Planetary Intelligence: Agiel

Planetary Spirit: Zazel

Deities: YHVH Elohim, Hera, Kronos, Saturn, Ea, Ishtar, Parvati, Kali, Hekate, Net, Ptah

Taste: Astringent

Stones: **Onyx**, **obsidian**, **jet**, apache tear, **bone**, **coal**, **hematite**, **black tourmaline**, garnet, black diamond, sapphire

Plants: **Aconite**, Americanstyrax, **asafetida**, asparagus, baneberry, barley, **belladonna**, black adder, black hellebore, bladderwrack, blue dogbane, boneset, buckbush, cramp bark, comfrey, **cumin**, **datura**, devilweed, dodder, **foxglove**, hellebore, hemlock plant, hemp, henbane, **horsetail**, ivy, jack in the pulpit, knapweed, knotgrass, lobelia, **mandrake**, mastic, morning glory, moss, **nightshade**, orris root, pansy, **patchouli**, **poke root**, poppy, **potato**, **rue**, scullcap, sheppard's purse, spinach, snakeweed, solomon's seal, spurge, St. John's Wort, **tamarind**, thyme, tobacco, tomato, turmeric, wild lettuce, wolfsbane, yarrow

Trees: Ash, beech, **black walnut**, cypress, **dogwood**, elm, **holly**, ironwood, **myrrh**, oak gulls, oak gulls, persimmon, chokecherry, **pine**, **quince**, rowan, **willow**, **witch hazel**, yew

Colors: Dark purples, gray and black

Birds and flying mammal: Bat, **crow**, black bird, **owl**, ostrich

Animals: **Goat**, ass, cat, hogs, mole, **mouse**, hare, mule, bear, ape
Insects, arachnids, reptiles, and others: Grasshopper, beetle, flies, gnats, locust, scorpions, black widow, toad

Water Animals: Crocodile, eel, shell fish, dogfish, cuttlefish

Mystical Beings: Ghouls, larvae, satyrs, basilisk, **gnomes**

Body: Excretory system, anus, bones, knees, joints, teeth, nails, spleen

Mystical Virtue: Solidification and Silence

Vice: Avarice/Greed

Antidotes to vice: Generosity and letting go

Areas of Influence: Death, karma, limitations, investments, career, solidification, discipline, learning, end of personal realm, bindings, boundaries, contractions, protection, invisibility, dealing with authority, self-discipline, administration, time, manifestation, formulating, grounding, order and organization, tedious effort and work, breaking unwanted habits, responsibilities, contemplation, endurance

General Characteristics: Organized, stern, responsible, self-assertive, cautious, down to earth, serious, austere, hard working, conservative, practical, reserved, quiet, self-controlled, disciplined, thrifty, exacting, patient, integrity, faithful, steady, reliable, industrious, persevering, traditional, orthodox, solitary, stable, efficient

Negative Qualities: Phobias, guilt, anxiety, pessimistic, melancholy, cold, impersonal, party pooper, self-denial, workaholic, slow moving, narrow-minded, authoritarian, constricting/restrictive, inferiority, insecurity, depressed, rigid, despondency, exhaustion, bondage, intolerant, critical, lack of confidence, doubt, aloof, sickly, strict, distant, timid, repressing anger, cheap, hording, and all around unbearable to be around

Sun

Metal: **Gold**

Sign: Leo

Day: Sunday

Sephirot: Tiphareth (Beauty)

Golden Dawn Grade: Adeptus Minor

Element: Fire

State: Hot and Dry

Humor: Choleric

Root Number: 6

Symbols: Breastplate, lamen, diadem, **candle**, **sigil/pentacle**, **lamp**

Tarot: The Sun

Day: Sunday

Year: 365.25

Olympic Spirit: OCH

Heptarchical King: Obogel

King of Jinn: Al-Mazhab (The Golden One)

Archangel: Raphael

Angelical Order: Authorities/Malakim

Planetary Angel: Michael/Hismael

Planetary Intelligence: Nachiel

Planetary Spirit: Sorath

Deities: Apollo, Helios, Sol, Shamash, Ra

Taste: Umami

Stones: Chrysolite, **citrine**, **jacinth** (yellow zircon), **topaz**, **sun stone**, **amber**, **ruby**

Plants: Agrimony, **alfalfa**, allspice, **angelica**, **barley**, **black-eyed susan**, borage, broom, **buttercup**, cactus, caraway, celandine, centaury, **chamomile**, **cinnamon**, cinquefoil, daisy, **eyebright**, **ginger**, **goldenrod**, goldenseal, Helen's flower, heliotrope, hibiscus, **hops**, **lemon**, lovage, marigold, mistletoe, monosodium glutamate, mouse-eared chickweed, peony, pimpernel, porcini mushroom, senna, rosemary, **saffron**, St. John's Word, sundew, **sunflower**

Trees: **Acacia**, **almond**, **amber**, ash, balm, **banana**, **bay**, birch, **cedar**, **copal**, **frankincense**, **laurel**, **lemon**, **vanilla**

Colors: Oranges, gold, yellows and reds

Birds: **Eagle**, cock, falcon, **hawk**

Animals: Lion, ass, **bull**, horse, ox, **bison**

Water Animals: Salmon, seal

Insects, arachnids, reptiles, and others:: Glow-worms, **bee**

Mystical Beings: Will o' Wisps, dragons, sphinx, phoenix, griffin, Pegasus

Body: Circulatory system, heart, blood, right eye, upper back, spleen, thoracic part of spine, arteries

Mystical Virtue: Awareness

Vice: Pride

Antidote to vice: Humbleness

Areas of Influence: Wealth, health, consciousness, strength, insight, understanding, wisdom, transformation, growth, purification, protection, life, guidance, arts, power, status, clarity, beauty, success, happiness, medicine, career success, employment, promotion, improving social status, friendships

General Characteristics: Bold, honest, noble, generous, honorable, strong willed, outgoing, defined character, self-respect, stamina, warmth, creative, inspiring, loyal, energetic, bright, compassionate, kind, sharing, generous, humorous, charming, charismatic, confident, lively, leader, protector, advocate, determined, dedicated, strong presence, courageous, positive, vitality, happy, analytical, straightforward, aware

Negative Qualities: Arrogance, head-strong, overbearing, brash, quick temper, burned out, stubborn, dominant, center of attention, overly self-conscious, megalomaniac, egotistical, impatient

Moon

Metal: **Silver**

Sign: Cancer

Day: Monday

Sephirot: Yesod (Foundation)

Golden Dawn Grade: Theoricus

Element: Water

State: Cool and Moist

Humor: Phlegmatic

Root Number: 9

Symbols: Crescent, **chalice**, **mirror**, **crystal ball**, bow and arrow, **ritual oil**

Tarot: High Priestess and The Moon

Day: 27.322 earth days

Sidereal: 27.3

Synodic: 29.5

Olympic Spirit: PHUL

Heptarchical King: Lumaza

King of Jinn: Al-Abeyadh (The White One)

Archangel: Gabriel

Angelical Order: Angels/Kerubim

Planetary Angel: Gabriel/Yehuel

Planetary Intelligence: Malkah b' Tarsishim

Planetary Spirit: Schedbarschemoth Schartathan

Deities: Anu, Aradia, Arianrhod, Artemis, Callisto, Circe, Diana, Hathor, Hekate, Hera, Jana, Juno, Levana, Luna, Selene, Shaddai El Chai

Taste: Sour

Stones: **Moonstone**, opal, **mother-of-pearl**, pearl, **crystal**, aquamarine, **selenite**, beryl, alexandrite

Plants: Acanthus, agave, **aloe**, alum root, anise, arrowleaf, bladderwrack, cabbage, calamus, camellia, clematis, **chamomile**, citrus, clary sage, coconut, cucumber, dill, duckweed, endive, evening primrose, fermented foods, fungi, gardenia, gooseberry, gourd, grape, hydrangea, **hyssop**, iris, **jasmine**, **lemon balm**, lemon grass, lemon verbena, lettuce, lotus, **mallow**, melon, milkweed, **moonflower**, moonwort, **morning glory**, **mouse-eared chickweed**, **mugwort**, orris, oyster plant, passionflower, peace lily, **poppy**, pumpkin, rose mallow, sage, sea holly, seaweed, **sensimilla**, star anise, strawberry, watercress, water lily, water hyacinth, white rose, wintergreen, yucca

Trees: **Banana**, **camphor**, coconut, **eucalyptus**, lemon, magnolia, maple, **myrrh**, **willow**

Colors: Silver, white and gray

Birds: Owl, **dove**, stork, duck, geese

Animals: **Rabbit**, **bull**, cat, **deer**, cow, dogs, pigs

Water Animals: **Crab**, clams, fish, frogs, **turtles**, shellfish, lobster, otter

Insects, arachnids, reptiles, and others: Snails, horned beetle

Mystical Beings: Lemures, ghosts, vampires, harpy, hydra

Body: Hormones, lymphatic system, stomach, breasts, bladder, womb, tears, saliva, sleep

Mystical Virtue: Reflection

Vice: Sloth/Idleness

Antidotes to vice: Zeal and dedication

Areas of Influence: Clairvoyance, cycles, intuition, peace, fertility, inspiration, emotions, receptivity, reflection, changing, glamour, unconsciousness, dreams, instincts, family, secrets, embassies, love, navigating

General Characteristics: Homely, gentle, relaxed, open, receptive, persistent, emotionally expressive, nurturing, caring, sensitive, empathic, generous, curious, magnetic, mystical, mysterious, playful, sympathetic, compassionate, instinctual, altruistic, psychic, fluid, flowing, connected, imaginative, poetic, charming

Negative Qualities: Weakness, laziness, overly emotional, moody, sad, slow, round-about, uncertain, hesitant, clingy, changeable, fickle, crabby, vanity, sentimental, lack identity, attached, daydreaming, lost in fantasy, gambling, restless, ungrounded, insatiable cravings, avoidance, indecisive, insecurity, self-conscious, mood swings, jealousy, envy, possessiveness, restless

Mars

Metals: **Iron**, **steel**, **nickel**, manganese

Signs: Aries and Scorpio

Day: Tuesday

Sephirot: Geburah (Discipline, Strength)

Golden Dawn Grade: Adeptus Major

Element: Fire

Humor: Choleric

State: Hot and Dry

Root Number: 5

Symbols: **Sword**, shield, **pentagram**, spear, **dagger**, scourge, chain

Tarot: Tower and Emperor

Day: 24.6 hours

Year: 687 earth days

Olympic Spirit: PHALEG

Heptarchical King: Abalel

King of Jinn: Al-Ahmar (The Red One)

Archangel: Kamael/Samael

Angelical Order: Powers/Seraphim

Planetary Angel: Zamael/Tharshish

Planetary Intelligence: Graphiel

Planetary Spirit: Barzabel

Dieties: Nergal, Ares, Vulcan, Elohim Gibor, Hephaestus, Agni

Taste: Pungent

Stones: **Ruby**, **garnet**, **bloodstone**, red jasper, fire opal, pipestone

Plants: Absinthe, a**safetida**, agaric mushroom, **basil**, cactus, calamus, cardamom, **cayenne**, chili pepper, galangal, **garlic**, horehound, horseradish, leeks, madder root, **mustard**, **nettles**, onion, **pepper**, pennyroyal, radish, thistle, **tobacco**, turmeric, **wormwood**
Trees: Ash, **black cherry**, **dragon's blood**, hawthorn, **nutmeg**, **pepper tree**, **pewen**, **pine**

Colors: Reds

Birds: **Hawk**, **rooster**, **crow**, **woodpecker**, **vulture**, falcon, owl, kite

Animals: Horse, bear, wolf, boar, ram, leopard, **badger**

Insect, arachnids, reptiles and such: Scorpion, gnats, lapwing, locust, wasp

Water Animals: Lobster, crayfish, shark, pike

Mystical Beings: Furies, chimeras, cockatrice, basilisk, **salamander**, werewolf

Body: Muscular system, blood, bile, gallbladder, adrenal glands, tendons, genitals, arteries, head, face, intestines, kidneys

Mystical Virtue: Energetic Movement

Vice: Wrath

Antidote to vice: Kindness and Compassion

Areas of Influence: Strength, courage, force, power, will, competition, alchemy, energy, vitality, confidence, self-assertion, sexuality, ambition, protection, breaking down energies, raw energy, making things happen, initiation, discord, wild passions, over-coming obstacles

General Characteristics: Ardent, powerful, willful, bold, holds ground, brave, leadership, fearless, outgoing, energetic, driven, honorable, ambitious, intense, confident, determined, enthusiastic, resolute, active, dynamic, independent, straightforward, spontaneous, speaks mind, inspiring, risk-taker

Negative Qualities: Impulsive, aggressive, angry, frustrated, destructive, confrontational, intimidating, quarrelsome, bullying, repressive, dominating, superiority complex, impatience, rule breaking, pushy, abusive, violent, restless, arrogant, reactive, rash, trouble-maker, opinionated, gambler

Mercury

Metals: Quicksilver, **aluminum**, alloys

Signs: Gemini and Virgo

Day: Wednesday

Sephirot: Hod (Splendour)

Golden Dawn Grade: Practicus

Elements: Air and Water

State: Dry and Moist

Humor: Sanguine

Root Number: 8

Symbols: **Caduceus, grimoire/ritual diary, stylus**

Tarot: Magician

Day: 175.97 earth days

Year: 88 earth days

Olympic Spirit: OPHIEL

Heptarchical King: Naspol

King of Jinn: Burqan (Two Thunders)

Archangel: Raphael

Angelical Order: Archangels/Beni Elohim

Planetary Angel: Raphael/Hisniel

Planetary Intelligence: Tiriel

Planetary Spirit: Tapthartharath

Deities: Odin, Loki, Thoth/Tehuti, Nabu, Ganesha, Elohim Tzabaoth, Hermes, Mercurius

Taste: Bitter

Stones: **Opals**, **agates**, alexandrite, **orange calcite**, **carnelian**, **topaz**

Plants: Alfalfa, anise, arugula, bayberry, betony, bitter melon, bittersweet, **burdock root**, caraway, carrot. celery, chamomile, chervil, cinquefoil, clary sage, coffee, dandelion greens, **dill**, dulse, **echinacea**, **elder flower and berry**, endive, fennel, fenugreek, **fern**, flax, forget-me-not, germander, honeysuckle, kale, **lavender**, lemongrass, **licorice**, **marjoram**, mullein, orchids, **parsley**, peppermint, **sage**, savory, scullcap, trefoil, uva-ursa, valerian, verbena, vervain

Trees: **Acacia**, **almond**, cassia, **cherry**, **filbert**, **hazel**, heather, **larch**, mastic, pecan, pistachio, sandalwood, **sassafras**, slippery elm, **walnut**

Colors: All colors and orange spectrum

Birds: Ibis, swallow, parrot, crane, swift, magpie

Animals: Ape, jackal, coyote, **fox**, dogs, weasels, ferrets, monkey

Insects, arachnids, reptiles, and others: Chameleon, cricket

Water Animals: Forkfish, mullet

Mystical Beings: Wyvern

Body: Brain, nervous system, senses, hands, tongue

Mystical Virtue: Truthfulness and Clarity

Vice: Envy

Antidote to vice: Contentment

Areas of Influence: Unifying opposites, rational mind, communication, commerce, knowledge, creativity, power of the mind, magic, discernment, innovator, invention, alchemy, interconnection, dichotomous, paradox, education, travel, siblings, medicine, eloquence, intelligence, sciences, divination, writing

General Characteristics: Versatile, mutable, eloquent, inventive, prankster, adventurer, lucky, agile mind, curious, provocative, dexterous, clever, quick, adaptable, intelligent, witty, articulate, bright, intuitive, logical, deep, socially networked, discerning, sharp, resourceful, persuasive, imaginative, shrewd, investigative

Negative Qualities: Cunning, fraud, perjury, theft, secretive, manipulative, boaster, liar, cheater, idiot, meddler, cherry picker, perverted, mad hatter, ambivalent, ungrounded, mental, frazzled, mentally lost, argumentative, muddled, confused, lost in the head, very opinionated, know-it-all, anxious, dwelling, fixated, mental exhaustion, lethargy

RITUALS

BETHOR **55**
HAGITH **58**
ARATRON **62**
OCH **69**
PHUL **72**
PHALEG **77**
OPHIEL **81**
BETHOR and ARATRON .. **88**
HAGITH and OCH **90**
ARATRON and PHUL **97**
OCH and PHALEG **100**
PHUL and OPHIEL **104**
PHALEG and BETHOR **109**
All Olympic Spirits **116**

This chapter deals with my ritual experiences, insights, practices and thoughts that arose while working with the Olympic Spirits. I have done four Arbatel Cycles. The first cycle was ten rituals long, and the last three cycles were seven rituals each. I include fourteen ritual notes in this chapter to give an example of my magical style and to share with you some of the insights and blessings I received.

BETHOR

Altar

- Blue Altar Cloth
- Candle
- Coal and Censor
- Tin sigil
- Topaz and Lapis Lazuli
- Elk wool
- Herbs
    - Cloves
    - Cedar sap
    - Oak bark

    - Marjoram
- My Tibetan Pipe with Jack Herer, Headband and OG Silver Haze mix

*Because of the way I have organized this book, I have moved some poems from each of the rituals to other parts, for instance, the first insight in this ritual dealt with inscribing sigils. I moved that poem to the sigil section of the Ritual Chapter.

Below are some pithy poems and insights that arose during my ritual.

After the Great Abyss there is solidification –
Patterns of Energies intertwined.

Clear the mind:
feel,
connect,
grow,
become,
In-Joy

****

This highlights the process of opening to the energy. First we clear our minds, then we feel the energy, actually touch in and experience it. As we progressively deepen our connection, focusing our full attention upon the planetary essence, we exchange energy and commune with the intelligences abiding within that plane, which in turn gives rise to deep insights, understandings and wisdom.

Through that process we grow – incorporating the higher frequencies within our mental matrix.

And of course, all the while we enjoy the process and energy. We are not trying to invite suffering and crap into our lives, but beauty, pleasure, joy, abundance, wisdom, and all that jazz.

The tools are not pristine,
always new
on display
dusty from lack of use.

They are dirty

stained
burned
worn
and used.

Like the tools of a seasoned carpenter,
they are chipped
oily
dirty
and worn –
though, always sharp and powerful.

You ever wonder why tree sap is an essential ingredient in most sacred incense mixes?

Trees carry the wisdom of our ancestors.
Our search for the Tree of Life is evidence of their importance,
as is the Druids and other traditions who honor them in their rituals and teachings.

Each tree carries its own energy and experience.
Just burning parts of the Tree imparts a little of that energy
knowledge
and wisdom into our lives.

When we work with stones
plants
animals
minerals
and metals,
we extend ourselves into the planetary realm we are working with.

Adding to those things we utilize images
numbers
colors
sounds
and what have you,
ever extending ourselves deeper into the planet's realm.

****

Part of working with these different objects is to help us connect with the planetary energies. First, we learn to connect with the energy via the simpler essences, and then, as our knowledge and experience grows, so does our ability to tap into and work with more and more of the energy.

HAGITH

With these stones (emerald and rose quartz)
we create a space for you to abide,
and with this metal (copper),
we ask you to arise –
to channel your energy into our lives.

And with these animals (rabbit and bull)
we give form to your essence –
a place for it to reside.

I pray that this is a good start to our relationship,
as I wish you to remain in my life.

****

We seek to attract the Vernal energies into our lives by using these physical objects to connect and resonant with her vibration. And depending of course with what we choose to use, will determine how, what, and which of her energies will manifest in our lives.

I personally like to use those energies that naturally resonant with me. As the emerald is my birth stone, rabbit and bull are both my totems, and rose is an herb I use in many different teas I make; it only seems natural to use those energies in my rituals. Adding of course different energies helps extend our relationship with the planets and widen our experience of working with them.

As a side note, don't use my calls and prayers. While that is standard practice when working with grimoires, I highly suggest you read and get to know as much as you can about each planet and then open yourself to that energy and allow it to come forth.

Trust that you are capable of connecting with the planetary spirits and trust in the inspiration that arises. That's what's important. It is not about regurgitating my words, even if they are beautiful, for that is my relationship with these energies. Instead, allow the energies to speak through you, and you will find as I have, that the wisdom has always been inside: Trust Your Self.

Naked,
we call you forth HAGITH,
we welcome you –
please come.

Unlike my predecessors,
I wish you no harm
no malice
no prison.

I welcome you here as a friend,
not as your master.

****

I found a resistance with HAGITH when I first called her. But after having stated that I wished to build a balanced and respectful relationship with her instead of forcing her to do my will, I felt her energies soften and open to me.

After that I found myself telling her what follows:

I wish to connect
grow
flourish,
to blossom into beauty
joy
and pleasure.

I want it all.

So come,
please come into our lives,
fill us with your wisdom
joy
and bliss.

We call you into our lives –
our hearts:
may your passion flow within us.

Help build our relations,
inviting joy, pleasure and beauty.

Deepen our relationship with the world and all that it encompasses.

****

While there is no set thing I go into ritual for, two things in particular that often come up in my rituals is seeking to invite those qualities of the Spirit I like into my life and banishing those things that I do not.

And I can tell you from personal experience, having that intention definitely increases the effectiveness of my rituals.

We invite your many gifts into the world:
giving and receiving –
May All B Blessed.

Make teas of nutritional herbs and invite the planetary energies into you as you drink them:
Be Nourished and Empowered

Jade was awesome.
There were a lot of things in my life that have tainted me,
much like the spotted jade piece I was holding.

Yet,
together we were able to clear away and see clearly what it is that is holding me back, blocking my way, distorting my vision. Now I see and understand.

We ask that those things under your domain:
skin, hair, hormones, emotions and so on,
be made strong
healthy
balanced
and beautiful.

That your grace
fluidity
and enamoring qualities be imbued within our lives.

Help us transmute –
transform our sexual energies:
that raw force of desire into fulfillment and bliss.

Help us dissolve your unsavory qualities that enslave
distort
and distract us from the Greater Pleasures of Life.

HAGITH had no patience for me taking notes.
She wanted my full attention, respect and affections.

****

In ritual I have a notebook that I use to record my insights, questions, practices, experiences, and such in. As I was writing down my insights I felt HAGITH's displeasure. She wanted my full attention – a Vernal kind of thing for sure.

I usually have this obsessive drive to record my insights as they arise because I have a tendency to forget them – at least – there is a fear that I will forget them.

As I worked with HAGITH I realized that this is an issue, as I have become lazy and inattentive. If we are fully present and aware, then there would be nothing lost, it is only when we are fixated on the past or obsessed with the future that we find our present moment slipping by.

After I stopped recording, I stopped having insights,
which was good,
for when we are running after insights and knowledge we sometimes have a tendency to get caught up in the mind and forget to be fully present in the moment – in the body.

HAGITH gave me the gift of enjoying the moment. During the ritual I slowly dragged the rabbit fur over my whole body. It was sensual and very enjoyable. After that I just laid down and spent an hour enjoying the sensations of the body without allowing the mind to take over and analyze, debate, think, and do what it does. It was a lovely finish.

As I closed the ritual I opened my arms and hugged myself while vibrating her name.

ARATRON

Crow
Obsidian
Pine
Lead

Harvest/Death
Obstacles/Restriction

Limits due to fear, self-doubt, weakness and lack of resources
Solidification
Wisdom
Facilitator/Solidifier
Boundary of personal awareness/perception
Protection
Consolidating Energy

Harsh
Real
Raw

My Saturn Medicine

The Willow and Pine

Take us to the other side,
let us come back with visions –
remembrances of Golden Times.

To the Kabbalist
you're solidification –
prior to manifestation.

The Great Father
The Great Architect
The Great Mold from which everything fills and is formed by.

****

The thought of the Golden Age came up. Why?

As I meditated on the Golden Age I thought about Saturn's placement on the Tree of Life and how that fits in with everything. Saturn is an amazing and powerful planet. While some considered it a maleficent planet, I do not. In fact, I have come to really appreciate Saturn as it helps ground my Mercurial Mind and direct me towards manifesting my visions.

Thank you,
you are right,
I do need to move on.

Thy Death is a blessing:
getting rid of the old –
welcoming the new

*This arose from my attachment to some things of my past. Some things that have held me down for a long time.

I imagine your sternness has more to do with disappointment than cruelty,
for we don't appreciate the blessings of these bodies:
utilizing the mind and body to their fullest potential.

Enjoying to the fullest
Thy Gifts of Life,
being fully Conscious and Alive:
that's what you bring to mind.

I don't want to fear anymore,
nor doubt.

Please, I invite your resolve,
your enduring patience and understanding.
I hear your call in the silence.

I'm Listening.

Help me systemize my Path,
creating a system of integrity and certainty:
A Grounded Path – A Deep Path.

To walk a Path you have to be patient,
you have to be cautious
aware
meticulous
and certain where you place your foot.

And you have to act –
to do the work.

"I am the Great Teacher,
the highest and yet,
most rooted aspect of yourself.

That's me.
And the Wisdom I impart takes you to the furthest reaches of that self,
that place before entering into the unknown abyss:
that spacious place of no-self."

****

Saturn is the furthest personal planet in our solar system. It is, in a very real sense, the furthest our sensory self can perceive without external equipment. In ancient times this was the encompassment of time itself – as Saturn is often associated with time.

As I asked ARATRON to help systemize my Path, the above teaching was my answer.

In some ways Saturn is one of the hardest energies to work with in our modern age. Things are moving so quick: instant cure pills are sold at every corner, instant meals, instant video streams – everything happens right now.

Saturn instructs us to be patient, cautious, meticulous, and absolutely certain before acting (sometimes even to the point that we never act – that is why we balance his energy with other energies).

It's great advice, but difficult sometimes to apply. And in my opinion, even more so when it comes to working with magic and growing up with magical movies that condition us to believe a wave of the wand and some Latin incantation is all that is needed to manipulate the physical plane.

To come back,
to yoke that pithy life before the growth,
the embodiment
the manifestation
the form:
That's Saturn

To come back and back into the moment,
solidifying it completely before letting go and enjoying the fruits of our labor.

Heaven has been at hand for a long time now,
and Saturn has been reaping his reward.

I ask of thee to help plant these seeds within the garden –
to grow these fruits within my life.

It's time for me to solidify my Path.

I offer you these herbs,
may they be pleasing to thy nature

I feel your energy.
I hear crying babies,
running feet.

I feel agitation
intensity
harshness
sickness
death.

Thank you for your austerity.

It would drive me crazy to bear all that by myself.

****

Currently I live in an apartment with my family while we save money for land. One of the things I love to witness as I work with energies is to see how it affects/effect the environment. There is no greater sign of the spirits in our lives than to see the differences within and around us as we call forth their energies.

In this case, I experienced the above.

Transformative power:
Great Alchemical Crow.
Divine messenger,
harbinger of death –
like The Death card of the Tarot,
thank you for transforming my life.

Dense
hard
compact
obsidian,
what have you to teach,
what weapon do you beat,
what has you surface reflection born,
what have you to show,
what wisdom will help me grow?

****

One of the driving forces in my rituals is knowledge. I want to understand, for in understanding comes wisdom, and with wisdom, comes many great blessings.

Thanks for showing me the proper way to approach you,
of calling
listening
and asking.

Thank you.

Visualizing your sigil,
offering incense:

"Thank You."

****

One thing I do throughout the ritual is continually give thanks. Not just for the energy, but the insights, the experiences and the practical suggestions I receive.

Gratitude is one of the greatest actions we can do to increase our awareness and power of life. It is also a great way to invite more blessings into our lives.

On Sunday set you intention
your focus
your light,
and let that guide you throughout the week.

I understand.
I invite and receive.
I come and commune,
sharing parts of ourselves,
we grow and become.

With sincere gratitude and a clear and focused mind,
stable
grounded
fully present:
we R here

Help strengthen our bones
teeth
joints,
help us to be strong and healthy,

to have a long and happy life,
growing from sadness
pain
and loss,
to a life filled with abundance and pleasure.

There's nothing wrong in asking for what you want:
ask for it and then accept it -
that is the surest way of bringing it about.

Just don't get fixated or locked in. That is one issue of Saturn. Be open to the many possibilities of Life, not just those you've imagined.

Saturn taught me how to ask for what I want and then to do those things that invite it into being

---

The ant has Saturn's energy.

Against all odds
external forces
or malicious children with magnifying glasses,
they are steady
methodical
committed to what they seek:
even to their own detriment.

The surest way to embody a planetary energy is to learn about them:
their stories
astrological correspondences
astronomical facts,
and so on.

Surround yourself with that energy,
invite it into your life,
then process and grow by dissolving those traits you don't want and solidifying the ones you do.

What actions
thoughts
beliefs
words
rituals and practices bring about what you seek?

That's what bears forth the fruit from the Tree of Life:
Now Enjoy.

If Heaven is at Hand and the Garden is within and all around us,
then the Tree of Life must be Too!

And that's a tool we can really use.

Use the system that is in place to accomplish your aims.

How do we know what we truly want?

If you can go through all your energies
Chakras
Sephiroth,
and see that they are in accord,
then I would wager that's something you really want.

OCH

We commence this ritual
fully awake
fully aware
fully present
fully here.

We invite the Sacred Sun to light up our lives –
enlightening our minds and strengthening our bodies.

Help us heal
help us be true
help us C
help us B.

We ask for your warmth
light
and insight:
looking within we come to our hearth –
R HOHM

To see clearly
openly
honestly
truly

to c what is,
to heal
teach
strengthen
and elevate,
ever rising like a tree to the sun:
that's what we seek.

Bay:
remove all sicknesses
diseases
parasites
and negativies,
clear the pathway so we may see and behold.

Be clear
up front,
say what you mean
and know what you want:

act accordingly.

Take care of yourself,
your hygiene
what you take in –
consume.

Love yourself.
Bless yourself.

Walk.
Drink living water.
Commune with the Universe and align yourself with its cycles.
Enjoy.

I have never used cinnamon in my offerings,
now I definitely will.

Isn't it a tree as well?

How awesome is that?

There's an exactness to pleasure,
a point reached that naturally catapults us beyond the limited self.

Thank you OCH for being in my life –
thank you.

Nothing missing
No memory lost
Standing in the sunlight
No shadow
Nothing unseen

PHUL

Poppy Tea

To drink of your energy,
not only inhaling your steamy essence,
but swallowing,
taking you in,
absorbing your being:
intoxicating
dreamy –
deep undercurrents of life.

Unlike sunlight with all its colors,
you give us hues,
mixing the Yin and the Yang,
we are born anew.

It's suffocating,
enduring this sickness:
it's madness to touch in with the shadow,
and yet,
that's what's needed to clean house and disperse the negative energies like the sun does to the morning dew.

Surrounded by this watery confinement,
disconnected and aimlessly lost within the mind and out at sea:
That's a scary place 2 B

****

The unconscious watery realms is a vast place. Much like being adrift on a little raft in the vast ocean, when we enter that place for the first time it is, in a very real way, scary. The thoughts that come up can be devastating, especially when we identify with them. One of the many lessons I have learned from the lunar sphere is not to identify with the images passing by. See them for what they are, illusions of the mind.

Sacred Heron,
airy energy of the Moon,
primordial patience,
precise as Artemis's arrow:
piercing your target – swallowing it whole.

Sacred Rabbit:
horny
fast
cautious
uncertain
flighty.

Little Turtle hiding under your shell:
watery reptile.

Gentle ones,
we seek your energies,
essences,
we invite you here in love and respect.

Please be with us,
help strengthen and guide us through the watery realms of the Moon.

Great Sea Snail,
your beauty draws us into your mystery, forever leading us deeper into the lunar realms.

Putting you to my ear,
I listen:
the Great Oceanic OM calling us Hohm.

Listening to your call,
I invite you in.

Using your key,
I open your door.

Visualizing your sign,

I infuse your essence within me.

"When working with me always go from the heights to the depths:
from birds
to mammals
reptiles
to sea creatures
herbs
stones
and metals:
This helps keep you from getting lost.

All the while,
hold to your intention,
be open to receive,
for with the me,
you never know what will come to be."

We inscribe your sigil –
your key,
upon this silver,
building a connection
a Pathway 4 2
to B-come
1

Left and Right are polarities:
Giving and Receiving are their manifestations.

ME
WE

B

I would like to sleep and have wholesome

beautiful
magical
powerful dreams,
that may guide me to the sea,
where the sun dips into the unknown –
returning Hohm.

The ego gets lost in there,
but those who do come back,
they have that look,
as if to say,
if only you could see what I sea,
you would understand.

You <u>wood</u>
under
stand

that's what a step is usually <u>made of</u>☺

I want to blossom and live in fullness,
to see many more moons rise and fall.

The Olympic Spirits are guides within the planetary spheres,
showing
introducing
and teaching us about them.

May we blossom and enjoy the fruits of life 2-gether.

Olympic Spirits,
while having a form and vibration,
are mirrors reflecting ourselves,
and so are colored by our karma and energy.

Unlike some,
I do not limit the Olympic Spirits to any one Chakra, but leave them open to all, so that their energies may unfold and empower us completely.

I don't want negativity,
that hurtful shadow,
that distracting desire in my life.

I want my mind,
my unconscious and all it subs
to be pollution free.

Be that polluting trash or thought,
and especially trashtalk, U C☺

I am so tired of all the desires.
I just want to B Here In-Joying.
Complete and Fulfilled to overflowing: that's what I want.

Complete Fulfillment:
not just spiritual but physical as well.

It is not about a sacrificed life
but a fulfilled one.

The Olympic Spirits quickly dissolve as we come to know their domain.

You ever wonder why PH sounds like an F?
Might P,
the Heavenly Part of B
be scaled with the ladder letter "H"

****

One thing I find entertaining and sometimes insightful is to play with words and letters. In this case, I have always considered the letter B to be an unfolded Circle (if you fold it on its back it would make a circle with a line through it, which of course could be curved to make the Yin/Yang). The top half represents the Heavenly Realms and the lower half represents the Earthly Realms. To me, the letter B is a great symbol for the balance between the two, and in fact, it is the letter of B-ing itself as it is for B-alance. The H of course can be seen as two pillars held together, or it could be seen as one rung on ladder. Seeing it as a ladder, it helps us climb to the Heavenly Realms.

PHUL – Full:

That's what I want 2 B.

PHALEG

I want your strength
drive
courage
endurance
power.

To be in control,
not be controlled.

To direct energy as I see fit,
using it like pepper to add fire to food and life.

"Inhale my essence
pull me in
absorb my energy
be my power."

Protector,
healer,
like a surgical scalpel,
cutting away the leg
to save the body.

****

Martial healing is needed when the soft forms of healing are not strong or quick enough. I always think of it as combat medicine and surgical procedures.

After the underlining identity of self,
I am the energy that enlivens it.

Unfettered

A powerful energy to break up the blocks –
little threads of Kundalini clearing the way.

It's best not to invite me fully in until you've strengthen the body,
increased your capacity to deal with a flood of energy,
and soften the energetic blocks, least I burn you up.

Without Mercury's direction and Venus's softness
I can be very destructive.

"Who am I?
I am the consciousness within this abode.
Why have you invited me?"

I seek power
strength
courage.
I seek your fire,
your flame
to ignite within me your essence.

To embody your energy to do with as I wish.

When you first work with me it is important not to exceed one hour, for that's just enough time to tap into my energy without burning up.

It's about the energy
not the forms.
The forms are merely keys opening doors to you.

After you gain entrance into my sphere and touch in with my energy, give it a few days to sink into your matrix and integrate with your being. Only then should you invite more of me in.

Out of all the energies,
yours stands out the most.

Sometimes it's not so much about learning
but embodying and experiencing first hand.

****

Unlike Mercury or even Jupiter, Mars energy is needed to be felt and experienced to understand. No amount of learning can prepare us for his energy.

"Unlike some instructions,
I like to meet in the process,
so draw me out and bring us 2-Gether."

Like any great grimoire,
I give you the keys,
it's up to you to put them 2-gether.

It's not a secret or puzzle,
it's just your Path,
and so, you have to discover on your own how to use those things given unto you.

****

Many esoteric writings are written cryptically. Sometimes this is because the author or authors are wishing to share, but not to give all the information. Be this for malicious, selfish or altruistic reasons, who's to say. Sometimes esoteric writings are cryptic because the author wrote the book in a different state of mind and so their thoughts do not come off linear. In other cases, the writing is cryptic not so much as to trip up the reader but to push them towards unraveling the mysteries of the writing itself, and in doing so, unravel the mysteries of themselves. When a writing is plain, it leaves little room for interpretation or personal growth.

No-thing can ultimately define the Universal Energy,
for it is a construct we conceive and build our world around and therein lies the energy,
not only in seeing it,
but believing it is as U C it.

****

It does not matter which system you use, it all comes down to you. In saying, as long as a system is complete and not full of too many pitfalls or contradictions, an Adept can find a way to utilize it towards their own fulfillment.

Personal Note: It's time to start exercising.

Telling myself,
"I don't need you desire,
your compulsive thirst for more,
never satiated,
always moving,
draining me of energy."

I direct the energy now.
Who am I?
I am Suba

And what does Suba mean?

One who forces a way – pierces a Path; a Comforter.

No,
I am not a beautifying energy,
but a strengthening one –

increasing one's vitality,
empowering your Will.

Blood stone –
rooting fire,
we ground your energy so that we may safely touch and work with it.

Woodpecker,
help me know where to peck,
give me strength and precision to strike and consume that which I seek.

Vulture,
harbinger of death and its transformation into new life.

OPHIEL

At the commencement of the ritual inscribe the sigil:

OPHIEL, hear us
we call unto you.

Changeable,
flexible,
seeing from every angle –
every perspective.

It can be exhausting flirting from one place to another.
So we have fun,
never without sharing some wisdom,
some lesson,
some annoying gift that often has great value.

Though my antics invite many a horrible experience:
rage

bitterness
jealousy
and so on,
the gifts that arise afterwards are often worth it.

****

When you read stories of the trickster, there are always those that react negatively – for who likes to be fucked with? At the same time, after it is all said and done, the tricks help us break away from our habitual ways of being and perceiving, giving us, for even just a moment, a new perspective on Life. That is worth more than all the politeness in the world.

Are we not to receive your wisdom and prosper from it?

Add acacia gum (Gum Arabic)
then lavender
before adding a sprinkle of marjoram.

"What do I care if you benefit or not?
I've got what I wanted and have moved on."

****

Mercury is forever in the present moment. Unlike Jupiter who is reaching into the future or Saturn who is stuck in the past, Mercury is in the here and now. Much like Venus who lives in the moment of enjoyment, Mercury is all about reveling/revealing in the moment from the intellectual side of things.

Attachment is not one of my issues.

It's not so much about some specific formula,
the right herbs,
the right amount,
for me you can use any herb
stone
metal
color
animal

and so on:
for where the mind goes, there AM I.

****

Unlike the other planets which have specific energies associated with them, Mercury can be invoked with any energy.

But as it is,
there was a void needed to be filled on the spectrum.
No one ruled orange,
and so,
on my journey through the spectrum people saw me there and thought,
"Hey, that's Mercury's home."

****

Mercury constantly moves quickly through the spectrum, so quickly even, that when we look at it we see Mercury vibrating within the orange spectrum.

So, we assume Mercury abides within that domain. Only, when we slow things down we can see that Mercury in facts moves through the whole spectrum, it just so happens that no other energy claims that domain, and so, the empty space appears to be Mercury's because that's what we perceive.

Astrology is all about understanding energies:
physical
spiritual
psychological
social
and so on.

The more we study astrology and look within,
the more we learn about ourselves and the world around us.

It's time to move on.

Bring in the smoke –
my energy,

encircle yourself,
be absorbed within,
don't lose you focus,
direct me wherever you go.

Why are fantasies and dreams a distraction?
Because they're limiting.

Learn to tap into the moment,
to check in and cash out before moving on:
don't doddle.

When the mind is fixated upon itself,
the body is freed and given a chance to awaken.

I don't want jealousy
bitterness
hatred
rage
confusion
cloudiness
subversion
trickery
covetous
vengeance
debauchery
or any other harmful,
hurtful
corrupting
or disturbing energy in my life.
Part of working with Mercury is to mentally state what it is we want and don't want.

Visualize yourself in the space you seek,
now abide there:
get to know it

see it
feel it
B IT –
watch as it arises in your life a little bit at a time.

So visualize it,
open you real eye and see:
for seeing is believing
and believing is being.

Be respectful,
honor your guest,
treat them as best as you can imagine,
offer your gratitude upon the coal,
open yourself,
inhale our essence,
and receive our energy into your life

or

if you are a goetic practitioner,
controlling and banishing those energies from your life.

Push those energies out of your life and into the triangle,
from there we can see,
know,
and understand what they are.
This gives us the means to forever banish them from our lives.

The seeds have been planted,
the energies have be sown,
awakened from the depths,
the energy will flow:
may it grow,
may it GROW

Apricot agate, what say you?

I am active between the heart and solar plexus.

I feel you activate –
polarize.

I am altering current.
Unlike Mars and Venus,
I am not solely directed,
nor am I like the sun,
radiating out,
I have my own energy.

I just ride on other's waves,
directing
shifting
moving
connecting
and screwing with them as I choose.

I am the fox and rabbit
the eagle and the dove
I am the badger
and the skunk.

I am little mouse
and worm.

The Tree
trunk, roots, flowers and herbs:
I AM HERMES

Night time rituals are nice in that we can sleep afterwards and see directly what kinds of energies we've invited.

Learn about your energy.
See what's around your house
your yard
neighborhood
park
city
forest,
see if you have any missing elements
planets,
become aware of your energy
your environment's energy
the Heavenly energy.

Invite in an agreeable way those energies you're lacking.
Don't be stupid and just open the doors to what comes –
for the world will come.

Use Discernment.

****

One thing I have learned in life is to be cautious when inviting energies into our lives. One way to understand this is to visualize the following. Imagine you live in the inner city and you open your door and put a sign up that reads: Come on in one and all. What do you think will happen? In the same way, don't be an idiot and invite a bunch of energies into your life without vetting and integrating them. I knew a guy who evoked a bunch of goetic spirits into his life all at once. Needless to say, I parted ways with him long before I could witness all the horrible things that were starting to come into his life.

Don't be in a hurry. Take your time to get to know one or two energies at a time.

Once you've opened all the gates
and learned how to integrate them individually,
the next step is to begin mixing the energies 2-gether.

How's the energy
what thoughts
emotions
sensations

memories
dreams
experiences
people
insights
situations arise?

Who am I to you,
and you to me?

The day is much like an opera house,
housing certain stories
areas
and energies.

The planetary hours are like the actors playing their parts.

The following set of rituals combine two of the planetary energies together. I added a few poor quality images of my altar before they commenced.

BETHOR and ARATRON

Learning how to balance the planetary energies is the next step towards becoming a Master Adept. It is not enough that we know the energies and can work with them, we must also be able to integrate them 2-gether. Working with two or more spirits at a time is the second phase of working with the Olympic Spirits.

My first ritual this cycle was Jupiter in Saturn's hour. Expansion and Contraction. How do we balance the two? (Balance isn't always found on a scale, it can be the right amount of ingredients in a dish or the point of gravity between two or more objects).

What can Saturn teach Jupiter and vice versa?
What's their relationship?

Part of working with these combinations is to learn about ourselves. At least, that is, what I choose to focus on. I also seek to invite health and prosperity, peace, joy, happiness, knowledge, understanding, wisdom, enlightenment and all that jazz.

An unfocused Higher Mind is as disastrous as an unrestrained lower mind.

It's all about what you choose:
that is as fair as it gets.

We might not be born with a platinum spoon up our ass nor live in a safe and nurturing environment, but we, as much as any, create our lives with what thoughts we choose to identify with.

It's all connected,
the Adept just pieces it 2-gether.

May the Spirit flow through our lives,
manifesting in the every Present Moment.

We Invite your Joy
Inspiration
and Support in our lives:

"Improve – Uplift," the voice says.

"Focus on the Vision of Life that's possible,
even if it is far in the distance,
and then start walking."

Finding some time to rest (Saturn/Saturday) is a good thing. Not only in giving substance for Jupiter's High-Mindedness to work with, it also gives us the time to rest and grow from our efforts.

HAGITH and OCH

The above images are from before and after my ritual.

Bison horns
Rabbit fur

Amber
Cinnamon
Rose
Lemon verbena
Passion flower
Rose quartz
Emerald
Sun stone
Topaz
Bison skin sigil
Copper sigil

Sometimes in life nothing works. My girls get sick, the neighbors are loud, the ritual area is trashed, the weather is hot and humid, the incense coal drops on the ground and starts a small fire, books start falling, tools are missing, everything is in disarray: what do you do?

I step back
breathe
relax
and let go.

Sometimes shit happens.

Breathing
Grounding
Finding my Center

I relax in that space –
it's all good.

Time for ritual!

As soon as I let go, burned some sage and smoked some herb, I was able to relax and avert one more distraction – I remembered to cover the fire alarm least the incense smoke set it off.

Nothing can tarnish the Golden Self,
only obscure it from shining through.

Inhail our essence
open to our energy
listen to our wisdom
embody:
4 we R 1

*And yes, I know that inhale is spelled wrong. For those who have told me I have horrible spelling, I agree, but not in this and some other cases. For me, inhaling is a sacred act, and so, I use the word hail to emphasis that point.

Slow down
Stop reaching
Let go
and just B In-Joy

That is so hard for me. To let go, to stop searching/learning, to just stop and B.

That seems impossible,
and yet,
here I am
saying otherwise.

This is the voice of Venus and the Sun 2-gether as 1,
speaking through this mind,
via this body.

This is R Energy,
take of our Essence,
enjoy.

For what better gift can there be than complete awareness and clarity while fully enjoying the blessings of life?

Use your hands to bring in our essence –
our smoke;
this offering you give us,
is a gift we exchange;

so ask and you shall receive,
receiving the answers you seek.

Just be warn,
there is part of you that will not like the answers you get.

Let go of those parts,
open to our energy and expand.

We evoke those things we no longer wish to identify with and invoke those things that we do: it really is that simple.

I've heard it said, "It all comes down to enjoying."
I agree,
only, it is a fine line to hinge your Path on.

It's much more advantageous to ground your Path on Complete Fulfillment,
where all levels of your Being are Filled.

It's all gifts.

We give in respect and gratitude to those energies/intelligences/spirits that have come into our lives and enriched us.

No one really talks about the obstacles,
the tests we go through as we connect with energies:
triggering a bunch of shit.

When I talk about evoking things,
that's the time to kick things out and invite things in.

When you've mastered the mind,
There B a God.

So break through the traps,

unclog those drains,
tap into the energy,
and clear the way.

****

This is very true. In most magical texts we hear a lot about the workings, what the spirits and energies can offer us, what amazing gifts we'll receive, but rarely do we hear about the tests and trials we go through when we work with those spirits.

Invocation invites the energies into our lives. When we do that, it triggers latent psychological issues, which in turn, invites a whole host of problems, memories, thoughts, emotions, external forces, experiences, and so on.

To become a Master Adept we must master our bodies and minds. That is the part so many fail to talk about. It aint easy to master ourselves. Anyone that says otherwise is full of shit.

Sugar is delightful –
addicting,
"It's just a little treat," the diabetic says.

Too much sugar
Too much salt

all the other tastes lose their identity,
and I don't know about you,
but when someone takes away my identity, I would become toxic to them as well.

****

This teaching talks about making sure you have a balanced planetary diet, which means, making sure you are consuming a little bit from all the tastes: bitter, astringent, pungent, sweet, salty, umami, and sour.

It also teaches us to make sure we balance all facets of our being: Unconscious (Moon), Mental (Mercury), Emotions (Venus), Conscious Awareness (Sun), Will (Mars), Inspiration/Imagination (Jupiter), and Body (Saturn).

It is learning to find balance,
not in pleasure or punishment,
happiness and misery,
but in the right amount so that the whole being and all that is, is fulfilled 2-gether.

****

Like making a cake, it is not about equal portions of all the ingredients, but the right amount of each that makes a delicious treat.

I watched a movie with my girls today.
The movie's message was:
even when you have bad parents,
shitty circumstances,
and the world is stacked against you,
you still have to choose the way you want to B.

That's Godly if ever there was such a thing.

Two hours past in ritual before I noticed the candle wax had spilled onto my green t-shirt altar cloth.

You don't need a golden chalice to drink from
or some diamond wand to wave around.

Your altar does not need to be made out of the arc
or grimoire pages wrought from the cross.

All you need is yourself
knowledge
experience
and understanding.

Having those,
Wisdom Arises/Arrives/Awakens Within.

So we got it –
how do we use it?

With control of the Mind
we shape it with our thought

and manifest it within our lives.

Like the Path leading us to that delicious pie
or a carrot to pick from the ground and eat,
we seek to enliven life by the Path we walk.

How do we know our Truth when so far the Path has been chaotic and confusing?

Slow down
pay attention
understand and listen,
doing that,
your doubts will dissolve and you'll know.

How do we work with energies?

Embody the thought,
see through its lens,
experience its energy,
and channel it as you see fit.

How do we channel it?

Focusing the attention,
aligning with its vibration,
and then subsume it in the mind.

How do we subsume?

When you no longer can see the energy as separate from you,
then it has been subsumed –
what need to call it anything else but U?
There's no separation

ARATRON and PHUL

Antelope horn
Crab shell found in Virginia
Myrrh for both Saturn and Moon
Pine sap from Arizona
Opium poppy I grew in Asheville
Selenite
Obsidian found in Washington
Lead and Silver sigils

Fear hides in every corner,
lurking about,
waiting to ensnare the mind and befuddle the senses.

Saturn is the root of self,
so naturally it would be in the root chakra.
Venus takes over all that sensual stuff,
and Mars sits nicely in the 3rd empowered and enjoying.
The Sun is at home in the Heart,
and Jupiter has an expansive voice to discover and express himself in the 5th.
That naturally places Mercury in the middle of it all,
and as for the Moon,
it is only natural to have her receptive energy receiving all the blessings from above.

It makes sense to solidify your Higher Nature before digging into your lower one.

So it's good to work with the Olympic Energies and learn to master the Planetary and Elemental Spheres before jumping into the goetic ones.

Then again, some say we should master our lower nature before climbing the stairs.

They say, "a bad foundation adds even more stress to our system when we go stepping out onto it, and ultimately, we fall in because our foundation cannot handle the extra energy and weight."

That makes sense when we understand how the Higher Planes bring in a lot more energy, and when your pipes are rusty and your nerve wires are shorting and split, bad shit starts to happen.

****

I come from both schools. We should aim for the higher planes while cleansing and strengthening our lower ones.

It's disrespectful when you don't smell and taste the Herb while inhaling. Like coming into someone's house uninvited, partaking in their food and drink without asking, and then taking a shit and not flushing or washing your hands before opening all the doors, turning on all the lights and leaving without saying goodbye.

Call it for what it is,
that's fear.
And here comes desire and all its attachments.
Over there is anger burning shit up.

Don't forget confusion walking around.
Jealousy, envy, and bitterness are whispering in the corner.
Hatred and doubt are knocking things down.

To control the mind we call things out,
seeing them for what they are.

We are the surgeon
explorer
master
friend.

Control the mind by clearly seeing what is,
then untangled and unattached it from those unbalancing and draining things.
Dictate what is allowed within the mind and what's not.

Any thought, emotion, energy that interferes in any way with what you seek,
strike it out of the book of life and out of your mind.

The circle is just a physical manifestation of our life
mind and energy;
as you grow upon the Path,
so your circle and sense of self grows.

The journey from the foundational elements
through the planetary spheres of the mind
ultimately leads us to the Great Mysteries,
and from there,
the Divine.

Know your Truth –
your Voice.

What is your Truth?

OCH and PHALEG

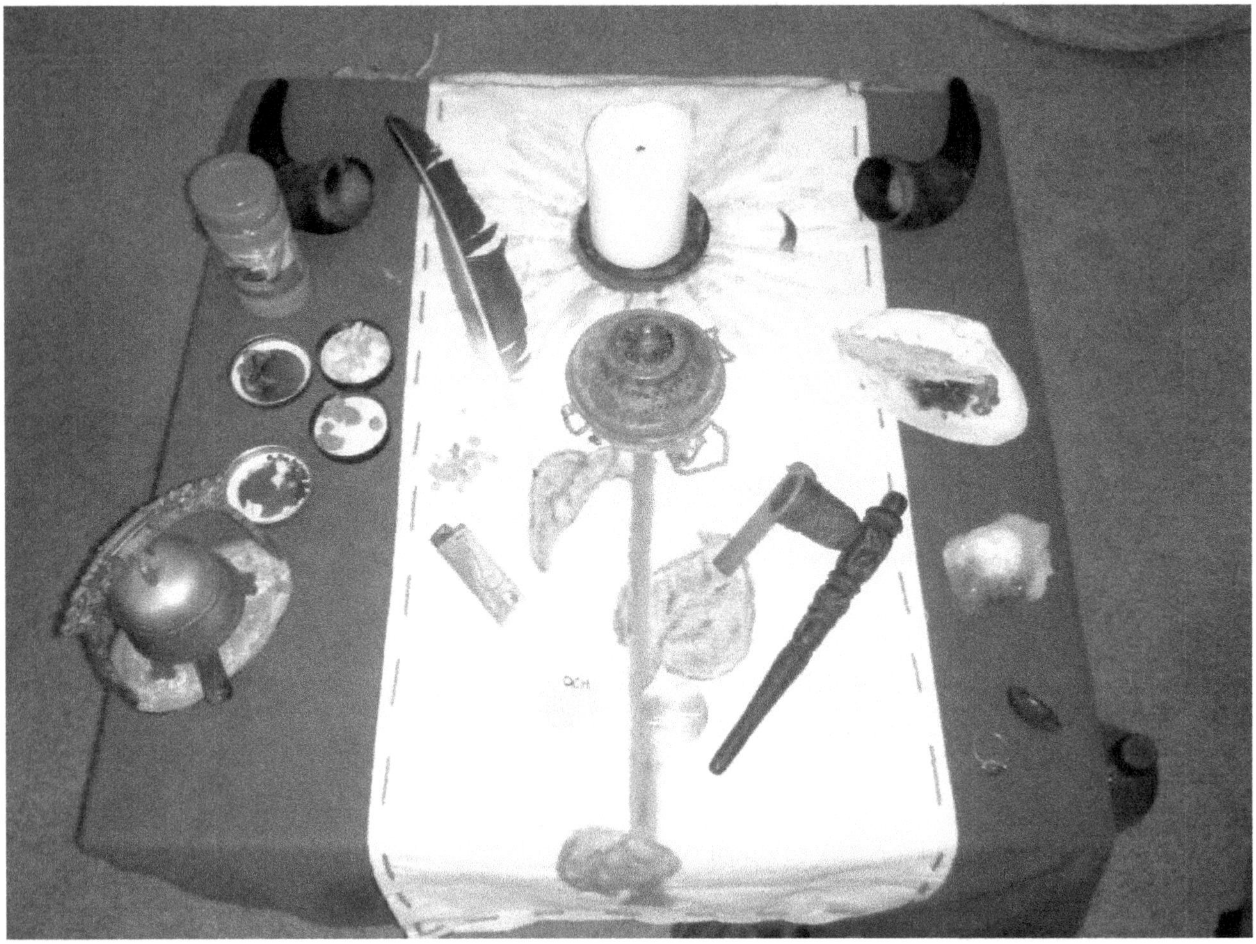

I originally planned to do this ritual during Mars's hour, but I decided to give my love a full body massage and have pleasures with her, so I missed my window. Even so, I am still going to work with Mars energy.

Vulture feather that came to me in North Carolina
Bison horns from Washington
Badger claw I bought through Amazon
Amber
Frankincense
Pewen sap I harvested in Washington (search *Araucaria araucana* – it's amazing)
Dragon's blood
Pepper
Garlic I started drying on Tuesday a few weeks back
Citrine

Blood stone
Carnelian ring
Bison skin sigil
Steel sigil
White sage I grew three years ago in North Carolina

The Sun,
radiant body,
always there –
I need only open to receive it.

Mars on the other hand is a force to be reckoned with,
instantly present,
vibrating:
lethal.

It's interesting to work with one planet during and within another planet's time and place – as I am now in the Sun's house during his own time, working with Martial energy.

Either way,
it's good for the Adept,
what better way to hone and control Martial Energy then within the Sun's Awareness.

Martial energy does not like to be pushed around,
but if you push his energy in a direction he likes to go,
he will not push back.

In saying,
give Mars a direction to move and then get out of his way.

Low magicians are those who still need to call upon external manifestations of the energy via spirits or through other objects of magic.

A High Magician is one who embodies those energies within themselves, no longer needing tools to get things done, all the while abiding in Joy. The Mind, that is what the Hermetics talk about, is clothed within the cosmos, which in turn, is clothed with God, which is again clothed within the

Ultimate Unknowable. Think it, and the Universe will conform to your thoughts.

Eventually all these energies, spirits, demons, angels, and so forth, become nothing more than a thought, an image and energy that is there whenever we choose to manifest it via our Wills.

I love astrology,
not so much for its predictive nature,
but in its patterns,
its perspectives into human and heavenly natures,
which continues to grow and embody our understandings of the Universe as our knowledge and understandings grow via the different sciences, philosophies, religions, arts, cultures, and what have you.

We learn to break down the Universe and the Mind into different domains, dispositions, approaches, expressions, and so forth, as we project our understandings out into the heavens, modeling them after our knowledge.

That is why it is so cool to study astrology from different people, for everyone has within them their own understandings and perspectives of life. With astrology they are given a framework to grow their understandings and mold it to their perspectives.

I suggest you utilize the Vulture energy and clean up all that dead stuff, then use the badger to tear up any stubborn energy that clings on.

Then, feeding and honoring the Bull,
enjoy the fruits and many blessings of Life.

It's never a question,
should we use magic to get what we want –
of course we should,
what a blessing.

The real question is,
are you willing to accept the consequences that arise from working with these energies before you truly understand them and before you truly know what you want on all levels of your being.

I would answer,

"I know what I want,
and as long as I can see it coming,
I'm all good with working with whatever brings it about."

I mean, of course I will study and find as many different perspectives and sources that I can to gain an understanding of these energies before I blindly call them forth. And of course, what I want has no negative impact on others, that in fact, what I want will benefit the world. So why should I fear working with any energy, when what I am seeking will fulfill us all. I do not have to fight with the energies, just subsume and gain momentum and strength, insight and wisdom, patience and wonder, and a million other beautiful blessings from them, and then of course, to use them as I Will.

Heaven is not some place inside or outside of us,
it's just a small little point where all things converge,
a point of silent awe –
that sound of Total Fulfillment.

Inviting the energies in,
we call upon the Olympic Spirits,
vibrating their names while reflecting the altar's light off the sigil's surface:
light striking our face,
receiving,
we open to the energy and embody its seed.

Interact with those manifestations/relational qualities,
grow in understanding and experience,
feel,
think,
imagine,
connect the dots,
connect the neurons and Wake up to your Divinity.

PHUL and OPHIEL

Lavender
Acacia
Eucalyptus sap harvested in California
Myrrh
Benzoin Sumatra
Selenite wand
Orange calcite I found in a Washington river
Apricot agate
Mother-of-pearl
Silver sigil
Aluminum sigil
Red tail fox fur
Rabbit fur

I found the answer to being wise:
just shut up and B –
for as soon as I open my mouth,
all kinds of stupid breaks free☺

Alright,
enough thinking –
it's time to call OPHIEL

The thing about allowing our lower natures to run the show is that they are always just looking-out for a limited concept of self.

Grandfather Sky
Grandmother Earth
Mother Moon
Father Mercury:
a child am I?

I am a boggart,
only able to see when someone defines me:
a horrible hell to live,
my only experience of the world is through fear.

So what do I C?

I am a succubus,
draining –
consuming desires.

Everything you use in ritual becomes a meditation tool, a connection with the energy that you have invoked. So when you sit during the day, you can hold the selenite wand, lay your head on the fox pelt, burn some incense, hold the sigils to the heart, visualize the doorways clearing and then partake in the ritual energy even while in the mist of your day.

Adepts build connections.

It's nice to know our planetary heritage,
for it helps us understand how we might best work with the mental planes.

In my particular case I happen to come upon it when the right energies we're alchemically infolded within my ritual.

****

Often times during ritual we come across triggers. Sometimes it is a sense experience that triggers us. I experienced a previous incarnation in a ritual I did with two others adepts: one coming from the Egyptian tradition the other from the Grecian. I was working with the Babylonian system during that time of my life. We were seeking to combined our energies to see what would happen. The Grecian Adept brought some wormwood, and when he placed it on the brazier I experienced being a French Adept. It was very powerful.

Other times spirits, actions, or energies can trigger an event, memory, insight, and so on. One time when I was working with a goetic magician, we had opened the Mercurial Sphere of the Greater Solomonic work and I ended up connecting with my HGA.

You never know what will occur when mixing energies. Experiment and find out for yourself.

While there are many ways to begin working with planetary energies, one nice and simple way to begin your relationship is to just look at your birth chart and see how they interact with each other.

Another thing you can do is check out what is going on with the planets in the sky right now. Where are they at, what are they aspecting, what about their transits to your birth chart? How does that knowledge deepen and expand your life.

Meditate and do rituals with them, and you will find great wisdom and opportunity to change your fortune: physically, environmentally, financially, emotionally, socially, mentally, energetically, spiritually, and so forth.

To me,
these energies are real,
and those spirits abiding within these spheres are likes wisps of knowledge, wisdom, and experience waiting to be tapped into. They can destroy us, or at least, harm us in some ways, or, we can learn how to harness their energies towards our aims and growth.

In my experience,
giving a name to such beautiful things/energies is natural, that way, when we want them in our life all we have to do is call.

These spiritual energies coalesce into particular patterns/wavelengths within our minds, which in turn triggers certain memories, thoughts, and feelings in such a manner as to affect/effect our being in particular ways.

As we gain experience with these energies/intelligences, we find, that whenever we call upon them, an energy arises within our space, our mental and physical space, and a communion unfolds.

While I do agree that these energies have a psychological effect, a mental and emotional impact, they also have a social and intellectual influence, and a hundred other things, all of which is valid. To call them just psychological energies just does not encompass all that they are. For energy can manifest as anything. When we connect with a pattern of energy, things happen.

Respect is one thing ritual has taught me.

Not only because it is a nice thing to do,
but it also shifts the energy of the ritual in a positive way.

It's so bright,
that moment,
that spark in the dark:
blinding.

Like a balloon popping,
a sneeze,
or any other all consuming thing that brings us to an open and pure state of awareness.

Hang there as long as you can:
invite it in –
B-come.

This is a form of Theurgic Union,
what Yogis call Samadhi.

As a personal note,

being an orphan
adopted
then rejected again,
and then spending much of my youth in prison:
I had a shitty start.

I have learned to neutralize many of those unwanted states of being in mind and body, but there is a karma to things, and it takes time to shift one's karmic direction. Those living patterns of energy within our lives have come because we attracted them, and so, things have to run their course before the new things we have invited can fully manifest.

Knowing our heritage does not damn us,
or limit us,
or define us,
it just gives us an energetic starting point from which we can investigate and interact with the Universe.

As you can see,
there is a difference between a High and low adept,
the lower adept just serves their lower natures,
be that in thought,
action,
or ritual.

A High Adept sees things clearly,
satisfying all desires in a balanced and uplifted way,
while avoiding being consumed, drained or defined by them.

The High Adept utilizes everything in their arsenal to achieve their aims,
just as the lower adept does with their desires.

The High Adept cultivates themselves,
not just for powers and knowledge (to know the ledge – the reaches of the mind)
but also in harmonizing their character, desires, needs, and so forth, in such a way as to achieve Complete Fulfillment, not just temporary pleasures of the world.

A low adept has a limited sense of self.

This does not mean they are not powerful,
for they can kill you –
that's pretty powerful.
They can mess with your finances,
identity,
legality,
they can even fuck with your life:
ruining it –
screwing with your mind.

Humans are powerful beings.
An adept,
no matter their pedigree,
can be very dangerous.

A High Adept though, rather than cause harm, seeks to uplift, empower and encourage others towards their fulfillment while being Completely Fulfilled.

The energy comes from overflowing – hoarding just blocks the flow.

I know people associate Arabic Gum or Acacia resin with the Sun,
and others with Venus,
I get it –
definitely.

I personally relate with it as Mercurial,
in that,
it is light,
subtle,
sweet,
and it is used in many things:
from pastries and food,
to incense and paint –
a very Mercurial/Alchemical thing.

I love my stone energy, particularly the mother-of-pearl a friend gave to me, to my orange calcite I found, to the apricot agate that came to me when I needed it. Orange Calcite to me is the perfect stone representing my energy, for it intermingles my planetary heritage: calcite as being lunar/watery by nature and orange, a Mercurial color. And the fact that it came to me while I was just sitting at a piece of land my wife and I wish to live on, next to a river, is just that much cooler.

As you develop on the path synchronicities start to happen exponentially. And not just as coincidences, but multi-level alignments that impact our lives in many different ways.

PHALEG and BETHOR

Woodpecker, Red Tail Hawk, and Vulture feathers found in North Carolina
Bison wool from Washington
Amethyst
Blood stone
Garnet
Lapis
Steel sigil
Tin sigil
Dragon's blood, pewen, juniper, and red cedar sap

There was a fight today in the complex, the police were called. There has also been an aggressive energy marching towards the surface. Earlier I got mad at one of my little girls. She had wiped something gross on me while I was studying the Larch. Needless to say, I said "come on" while slapping my leg with my fingers to emphasis my anger, and really feeling it.

Mars is a powerful force to tap into. Force being just one way in which energy is expressed.

****

I mention these things to show how the energy was effecting my environment. Time and again I hear practitioners complain that they are not able to see or feel the energies and spirits they are calling forth, all the while, they complain about a bunch of stuff happening in their lives: that's the energies and spirits doing their thing.

This is a wacky ritual.
Talking about my day conjured up the memory of the Larch.
All of a sudden I wanted to connect with and experience the energy myself –
to know it directly.

****

I use to depend on others to tell me what energies were. For instance, if I wanted to connect with an element I would research as many different sources as possible to see what other's had said about the different plants and minerals that were connected with that element. And then I would take it for granted that their energy was in sync with mine, and so, I would not question their correspondences.

The only problem was, sometimes their energies did not resonant with me, that in fact, their correspondences were counter to my own.

While I still research and seek out what others have to say, I do not depend on, nor even agree with them all the time. Even so, I still feel it is beneficial to learn from others as it gives us greater perspective, and sometimes, we even learn something☺

Larch

I understand,
your soft needles invite vernal energies,
your deep red veined bark and your ability to handle a little bit of fire conjures Mars,

and your height reaching into Jupiter's realm definitely brings to mind your traditional associations.

But your quickness of growth,
and your ability to be in all realms reminds me of Mercury.

As for Moon's connection,
well,
for an evergreen to shed its needles –
that's pretty loony if you ask me☺

When Mars hits you,
it comes on strong
hard
direct
heavy
and all encompassing.

It is good to have a direction you want to send it,
otherwise,
you will find yourself at war.

From the Elk's Eyes

Holding the wool in my hand,
smelling,
inhaling the elk's essence,
I hear that tapping
ticking
pecking of the woodpecker.

I love to watch the hawk fly down
striking the earth with her talons:
ripping flesh.

And the vulture reminds me of how short life is,
so I cherish it,
give thanks,

and enjoy the blessings while they last.

From their eyes

Vulture salivates
awaiting his meal.

Woodpecker flies
pecks
pecks
pecks.

Hawk thanks Elk for shaking things up,
little snake
prairie dog
squirrel,
giving thanks,
she dives in for her meal.

What does that teach me?

That this incarnation comes to an end,
that there are many things to distract and consume our energy and focus,
and that we should take heed and use every moment/opportunity we have to further our intentions – even if that's just about jumping into Life and enjoying yourself in a healthy and uplifted way.

****

While I was taking in the Elk's energy I had a vision from its eyes, seeing and experiencing the world from its perspective. The Vulture awaits it death, the woodpecker is oblivious of it, the Hawk is a powerful opportunivore.

Woodpecker

"I might be a little bird,
but my red head lets hawk and other things know to watch out for me,
for I will fucking poke out their eyes:

I am deadly accurate,

and I'll hear you coming as soon as you look my way.

I am mother fuckin' Wood-pecker, bitch."

That's how I imagine a modern human expressing woodpecker energy would be like.

Working with animal totems is intense,
for we literally open ourselves to their essence –
expressing it via our lives.

And animal totems are wild.
They are not like our domestic breeds,
they don't fuck around
and they will as soon eat you as help you.

It is a powerful
wild
intense,
and sometimes even violent expression of energy.

It can be a battle at first.

The surest way to find a balance and work with totemic energies is respect, honor, and having a genuine interest in the animal's way and wellbeing.

Imagine,
animals, trees, insects –
they're all alive:
breathing
swimming
running
flying
diving
enjoying
and yes,
fighting
striving

hungering
worrying
fearing
and so much more.

Garnet,
I seek your strength
endurance
and energy to touch in with my pain and move it towards healing and vitality.

I want to be strong
healthy
vibrant
energized.

Garnet Speaks,
"To do that you have to take responsibility for your healing."

Mars is all about action and energy.

If you do not have a directive/aim/intention,
or at least an outlet,
his energy will tear you up.

Wednesday during Mercury's hour inviting all of them

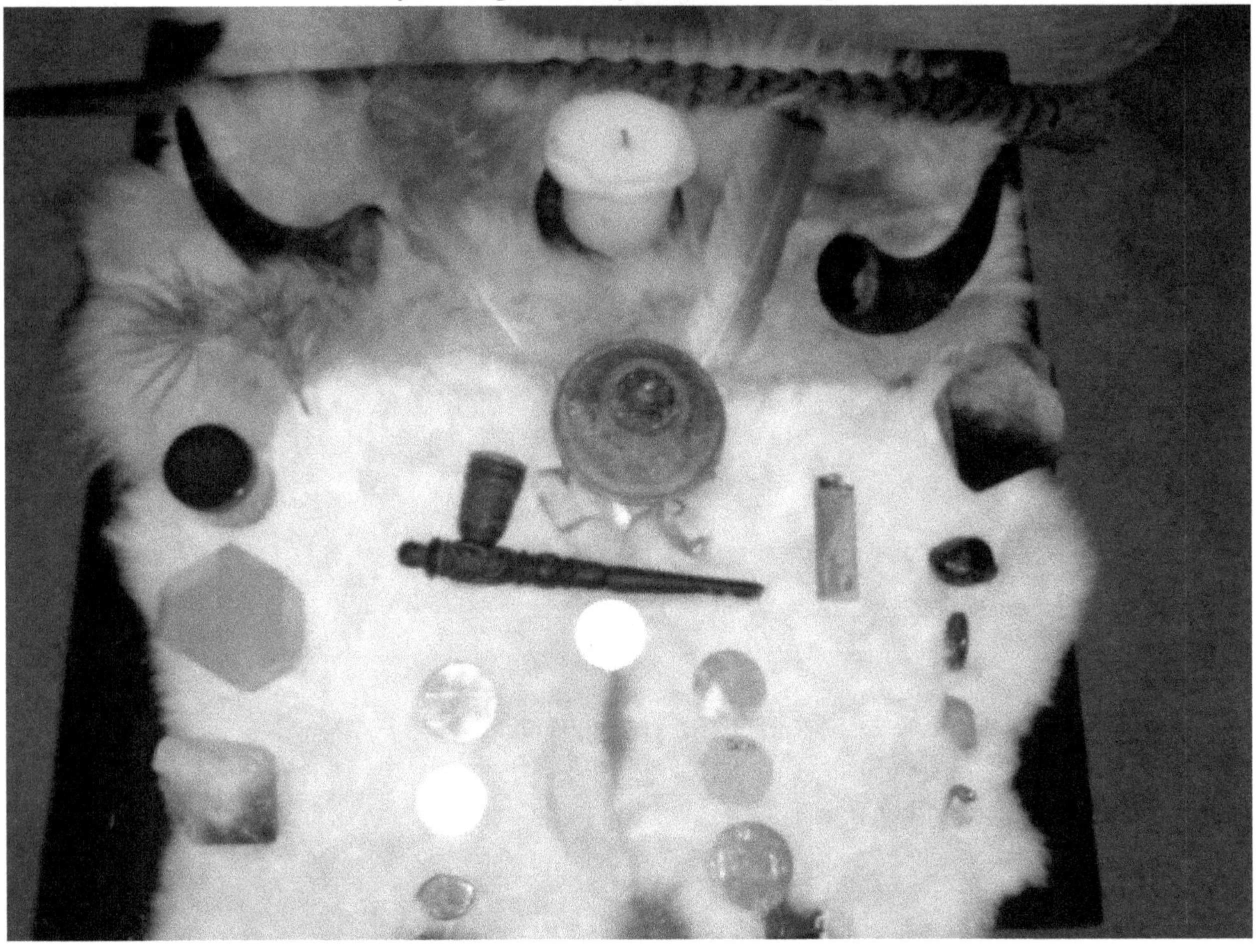

Mercury in the center.

Solidification at my left hand,
rarifying at my right,
one contracting into matter,
the other,
expanding into energy:
a spectrum of sorts☺

Fox pelt
Rabbit pelt
Bison horns
Hawk feather

Dove feather
Antelope horn
Elk wool
Planetary incense mix
Quartz
Amethyst
Blood stone
Orange calcite
Emerald
Rose quartz
Spotted jade
Citrine
Obsidian
Steel, tin, aluminum, silver, copper, lead, and bison skin sigils

---

Venus on the left	Mars at the right
Unconscious Moon	Conscious Sun
Saturnian body	Jupiterian Mind

and the Mercurial Self keeping it all 2-gether.

Stone Meditation

Orange calcite over third eye
Obsidian at my feet
Rose quartz on my groin
Blood stone on my gut
Emerald over my heart
Quartz in left hand
Citrine in right hand
Amethyst overhead,

let the energy flow
the spirit grow
and mind and body k<u>now</u>:
life is all about right here and NOW.

Giving
Receiving
Enjoying
Being

To the East I am Open and ready to receive
To the South I am Aware and ready to perceive
To the West I am Experiencing and ready to conceive
To the North I am Born and ready to transceive

One of my Tribe's Songs

I can hear the voice of Grandmother calling me (2x)
She says
wake up (2x)
Lisss-n Lissss-n (2x)

May the Rivers all flow Free
May the Mountains grow unspoiled
May the Trees Tall
May the Air be Pure
May the Earth B shared by ALL(2x)

I can hear the voice of Grandfather calling me (2x)
He says
wake up (2x)
Lisss-n Lissss-n (2x)

May the Rivers all flow Free
May the Mountains grow unspoiled
May the Trees Tall
May the Air be Pure
May the Earth B shared by ALL(2x)

I can hear the voice of our Grandparents calling us (2x)
they say
wake up (2x)

Lisss-n Lissss-n (2x)

May the Rivers flow Free
May the Mountains Grow
May the Trees be Tall
May the Air be Pure
May the Earth B shared by ALL(2x)

Jade was awesome.
There are a lot of things in my life that have tainted me,
much like the spotted jade piece I was holding.

Yet,
together we were able to clear away and see truthfully what it is that is holding me back, blocking my way, distorting my vision. Now I see and understand.

The real work is not the ritual,
it is in-between the rituals --
applying those things we have learned in our daily lives.

Just because we do not have time to work with each individual energy in a ritual, for instance, all the stones, metals, herbs, totems and things, does not mean we should get discouraged. Sometimes we only have a moment to connect with and learn/experience through one or two energies. Even so, all the other energies are part of the conversation, part of the ritual.

Opening ourselves to see from multiple different perspectives is a great blessing in life.

Second ritual with all of them from my second Arbatel cycle

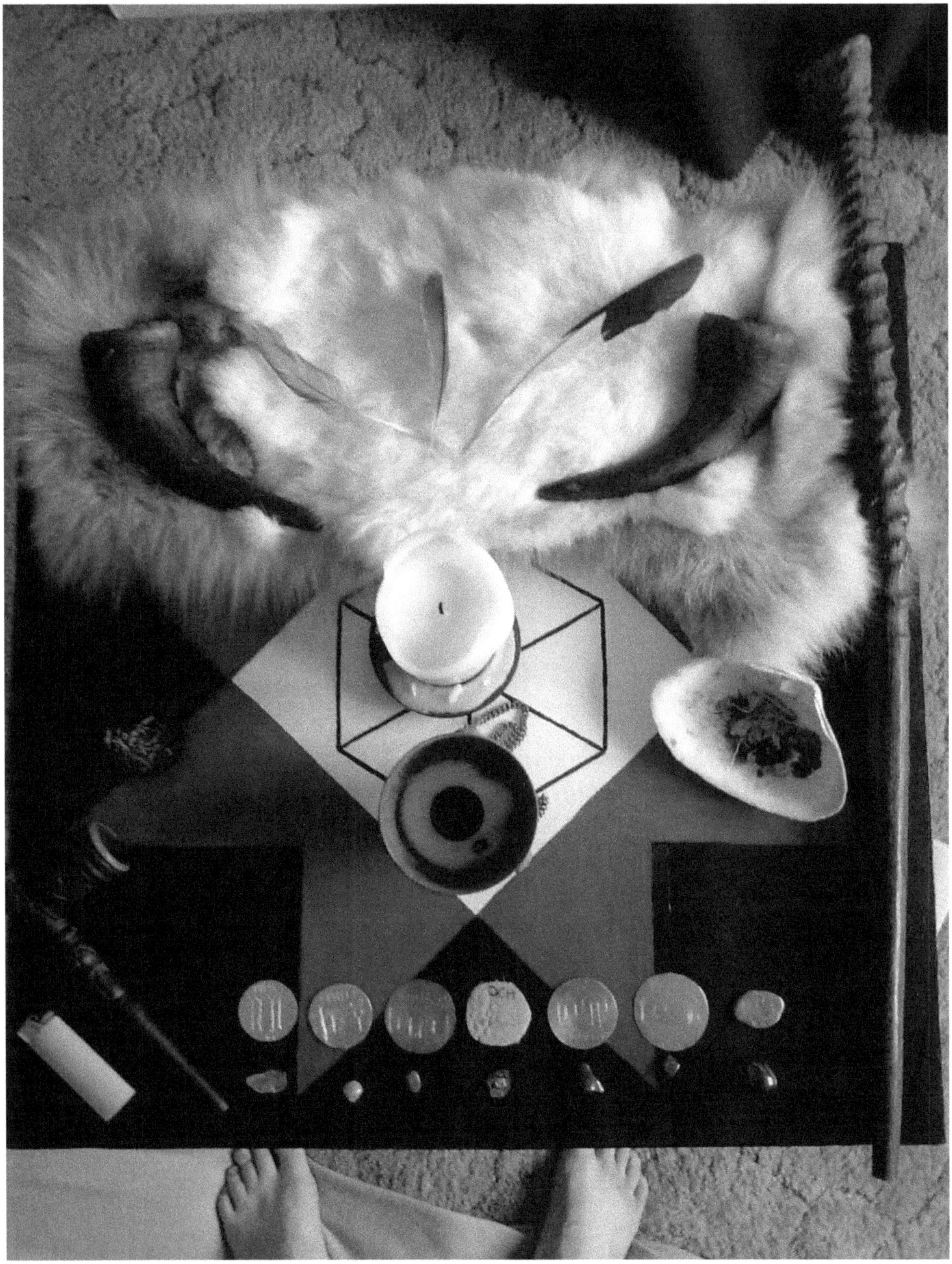

Fox pelt
Rabbit pelt
Bison horns
Woodpecker feather
Dove feather
Blue Jay feather
Antelope horn
Planetary incense mix
Mother of Pearl
Apricot Agate
Emerald
Blood stone
Topaz
Lapis
Obsidian
Steel, tin, aluminum, silver, copper, lead, and bison skin sigils

---

What have I come here for?

To finish another Arbatel Cycle.
To invite prosperity,
balance,
harmony,
joy,
and all the other blessings in life.

Connecting and embodying the Olympic energies in my life.

Mars – I **Want** your strength, vitality and energy; not just physically, but your inner strength, courage and power as well

Venus – I **Desire** harmony, pleasure and grace

Mercury – I **Seek** clarity, insight, understanding and connection

Moon - I **Open** to your abundance, fluidity, integration, changeableness and peace

Saturn – I **Will** my reality into Being

Jupiter – I **Extend** to all levels of B-eing

Sun – I **AM**

It's not about keeping the incense smoking,
but about offering our gifts,
taking in the essence,
and infusing ourselves within the planetary sphere.

When we find ourselves being drawn out of the sphere,
we again offer our incense and go back in.

Align the Body, Mind and Heart:
Only then can the Earthly and Heavenly Energies Connect and B 1

Just because we do not see the results of our chosen aim right away does not mean there is not a lot more being offered in the present moment – don't limited yourself to just those things you seek.

In other words, don't get fixated on what you want and how you want it to happen. Set the intention, send out the energy, and trust that what you have done is sufficient to accomplish your aims, and move on.

R you ashamed of these things?

Is it doubt
fear
attachment?

R U Con-F-lict-ED?

What is holding your back?

There is no-thing wrong with wanting it all.

Thanks Herbs and Trees
Stones, Metals and Things.

Thank you Living Ones,
those that run,
swim,
burrow,
and fly.

Thank you Great Spirit.
Thank you Mother and Father and all your Children.

Thank You.

Lapis,
so lofty,
so elevated,
the heavens are reflected upon the ocean's surface.

Blood stone,
blood and toil,
veins of life and energy.

Topaz,
wise
clear
vibrant,
bringing clarity to what's past and focus to what is near.

Mother of pearl,
delicate,
subtle,
gentle,
ephemeral,
colors swirling

shimmering within the Iye.

One way to invite the energies in a nice and balanced way is to add them to a potpourri and hang them around the house. This is also a way to clear and purify negativity from your life.

Silver – how to receive and reflect.
Aluminum – how to interconnect, while looking from many perspectives.
Copper – how to encompass and enfold; to delight from within.
Gold – need some. Please solar energy, come into my life with your abundance, clarity, healing and wisdom.
Tin – light, airy, rust resistance, open, calming to the mind, inviting stillness, clarity and farseeing.
Lead – heavy, dense, absorbing more light than giving off; taking all that you can; cold

---

I am the chaotic void –
chaos churning within the unconsciousness.

I am the experience –
the mind that recognizes and understands.

I am love –
the enjoyer and the enjoyed.

I am the sun –
the embodiment of consciousness.

I am the creator and destroyer of all that is.

I am wisdom incarnate.

I am Death.

The key to fulfillment is to actually shift the energy and align ourselves with what we want in the here and now: that's the only way to bring it about

---

It does not matter what you do later,
what matters is what you do now.

Waiting for another life is self-defeating,
do what you can to invite joy and all the other good stuff into your life right now

---

Don't get lost in the details,
focus on the energy itself:
does it invite what you seek?

If it does, then get into the details and allow it to blossom in your life.

Where there's no ego to hold onto,
there's Bliss –
flowing energy with no resistance.

Settle down,
breathe,
find your center,
your ground.

Breathe
Relax
Let Go
Open.

Breathe in the moment
Be Fully Present
Enjoy

Now begin your ritual

It's all about attention:
what we focus on,
what we desire,

fear,
believe.

R attention defines us.

Consciously it's what we point towards,
what interests us –
be it for substance/survival
pleasure/pain
wanted/unwanted.

Unconsciously it is our drives,
conditions,
programs,
those patterns we've adopted –
identified with.

Learn to focus,
rest the mind,
feel the sensations,
build the energy,
then let go –
feel the flow and grow.

As we light the candle,
we are inviting the energy to awaken,
inviting the spirit into our circles –
into R Lives.

We are not resisting the energy,
we are opening to it.

As the light shines,
so does our awareness,
becoming bright and clear –
focused and near.

We bring that light into the moment
and we see what's there.

The light is a symbol of Truth
Clarity
Transparency
Warmth
Love
Compassion
Passion
Intention
et cetera.

It creates an ambience,
a space where light and shadow can dance and know one another.

Don't get caught in routine:
don't allow the rituals to become common place,
to allow the mind to wonder,
get lost,
confused,
distorted while in ritual.

Sharpen the focus and bring your complete awareness to what you are doing.

See the Sacred,
the magic in all things

Invite the mystery into your life.

Remember to be thankful –
to be grateful for all that you have and B.

APHORISM MEDITATIONS

Principles of Magic 129
Microcosmic Magic 136
Olympic Magic 139
Hesiodiacal and Homerical Magic 147
Romane, Sibylline, and Druidic Magic .. 154
Pythagorical Magic 162
Apollonian Magic 172

The following chapter is a record of my meditations on the Arbatel's Aphorisms. While the Arbatel itself has distinguished nine tomes, only seven are introduced through the Septenary Sections. Each Septenary offers some principles of magic from each of the above magical systems. In a future work I will talk about the last two Tomes: Hermetic and Henosis.

If you are looking for the actual magical practices from these systems, you'll need to look elsewhere. While the author of the Arbatel labeled these Septenary sections after different Grecian magical systems, they do not, in fact, have much to say on any one of them. The only Septenary that offers magical workings is the third: Olympic Magic. What each Septenary does offer though, are the basic principles of magic that lead towards Theurgia.

First Septenary (Principles of Magic)

1	2	3
Be Fully Present and Aware Discernment Grounded Balancing Receptive	Know Self Be Self Enjoy	Always Be True to Self. Avoid unbalancing and depleting energies. Embrace each moment as your last.
4	**5**	**6**
Be Open	Love – hate and anger	Conserve Energy

Don't waste time Be Patience Loving Kind Compassionate and Wise	Faith – fear Joy – boredom and sadness Understanding – Ignorance Contentment – depleting and insatiable desire Self – Attachment	Reflect Grow
7 Listening Trusting	**8** Creating Enjoying	**9** Everything has a use A teaching An energy An essence A relationship
10 Watchful Inviting Letting Go	**11** Intentional Focus Introspection	**12** Focus on Keter Reside in Malkut Abide within Tiphareth: Radiating as 1

"Know and Act Accordingly"

The first three aphorisms are about being fully present, paying attention, knowing what we really want, not compromising, all the while, being true and loving to ourselves by avoiding those things that deplete or cause us harm.

The second three are about the actions we take in preparation for the magical operations. Not wasting time or energy, doing everything we can in our power to invite those things that fulfill us, and letting go of all those things that don't fulfill us.

The next three shows us the process of mastering the Arts and those things we have to work with.

The last section instructs us to be watchful, present and fully aware, while enjoying the Fruits of the Tree.

We consume its Seeds Within,
Sprouting

Growing
Nurturing
Loving
Embodying –
We are the Tree of Life:

Here,
have a taste.

What do you Think?

Calls

As with all great treatise on magic, philosophy, poetry, religion, and other such spirited matters, we invite the energies and intelligences that best suits our endeavor:

My Invocation

I call upon God and Goddess –
Father and Mother,
I call the ancestors
the spirits of the winds
fires
waters,
the spirits of earth and sky.

I call upon the Great Teachers
Guides
Protectors

May you assist us in our work
and may the fruits of our labor bring fulfillment to all those who taste.

1

Be attentive
Pay attention
Be fully present

Use discernment to know what bears forth good fruit and what invites sickness.
Know what invites joy and abundance
and what invites disease
depletion
and death.

Center the mind
Balance the body

Be Open and Receptive

Witness reality unveil,
witness the energy flowing,
experience it growing.

2

In the first aphorism we touch in with the Self,
that highest projection of the ego:
that event horizon –
that dazzling light surrounding emptiness.

Now we focus all our attention and energy upon that center-point/Self,
and experience the fluctuation between being and non-being:
Knowing Oneness.

In other words,
find your highest sense of Self
and point in its direction.

Embody its qualities
characteristics
energies
perceptions
and so on.
Live, Enjoy and Be Blessed

3

Always Be True to Yourself.
Avoid unbalancing and depleting energies/people/etc...
Embrace every moment as if it were your last.
Bless and Be Blessed.

4

Be open to truth no matter what.
Don't waste your time on fruitless Paths.
Be Fully Present and Enjoy.

Be Patient
Loving
Kind
Compassionate
Understanding
and Wise

5

Where Love is,
hate and anger cannot abide.

Where Faith is,
there is no fear.

Where Joy is,
boredom and sadness are nowhere to be seen.

Where Understanding is,
ignorance cannot reside.

Knowing Self
and Experiencing beyond it to the Oneness of All,
attachments dissipate,
for why would we hold onto a stale piece of gum when a candy store awaits?

6

Don't just blow through things in life,
for that is little better than not experiencing at all.

We don't guzzle fine wine,
not only would it hurt,
but,
what a waste.

In the same way,
be fully present and enjoy what is,
and as for those things you learn along the way,
reflect upon them,
allow their knowledge and wisdom to grow within you.

7

When you're stuck
conflicted
and find yourself in shit's creek,
listen to me,
hear that Voice inside,
that echoing chamber of the Divine:
Listen,
open yourself to the wisdom that lies within you
and you will be filled to overflowing.

Believe in yourself,
for I AM U.

8

While it is foolish to say we create it all,
at least,
from the perspective of the unconscious consensus,
it is true that we are Gods/Goddesses,
creating our lives from the inside out.

9

All things,
from the most rarefied energies
to the densest,
have wisdom to share –
something to give.

It's up to the Adept to determine what that is.

10

Be every Watchful/Aware,
align yourself with those things that invite what you seek,
and disengage,
dissolve,
and let go of all those things that interfere with your Path's direction.

Take stock once in a while,
check in,
adjust when needed,
and continue enjoying yourself as you journey towards deeper and more encompassing experiences of B-ing.

11

If you want something,
you got to keep your focus on it.
The more you want it,
the more attention you give to it.

If you want Divine Wisdom,
you have to focus on the Divine.
The easiest,
closest aspect of the Divine resides within and all around us,
so be fully <u>present</u>
and enjoy this <u>gift</u>.

Thanks Turtle☺

Don't get caught up on the powers,
for they are just signs that you're on the right tract.
If you get fixated on the sign,
you'll miss out on all the fun.

Focus on Keter
Reside in Malkut
Abide within Tiphareth:
Radiant 1

Second Septenary (Microcosmical Magic)

12	13	14
Dissolving Doubt Know Truth Believe Abide within that Truth	B Self – It's Y<u>ours</u>	2 B 1 Focus on the Good

"B-come Self"

Doubt has been one of my greatest challenges.

It is easy for me to see its root in my early childhood. Tossed from one family, facility, to another. I was the chameleon, a most unconscious totem of mine. I conformed to everyone's expectations, so extensively so, that I had to unravel the mystery of my personal identity even before I could address the ego.

Needless to say, over the years I have come to recognize my Highest Truth.

The closer we get to embodying our Truth,
the less doubt and darkness there is.

12

It's easy to fall into doubt when we come into these bodies, for as we sink into the lower vibrations things get darker and denser.

Know your Truth
Believe in yourself
Live accordingly.

When you are aligned with your Truth,
doubt will disappear.

And what is our Truth?

We discover it on our journey towards Fulfillment.

I think there is a mistake,
true knowledge doesn't come from hearing,
but from listening and understanding and applying what we've learned in our lives.

When we live this way,
we are Wise –
there is no doubt in that.

When we truly know what fulfills us,
and we direct all our attention and energy towards that,
there's no doubt that the Voice within will direct us towards that full-filled experience in everything we do.

The catch is, we have to listen - and the hard part – doing.

13

When you touch in with your True Self
Higher Self
Guardian Angel
Godly Spark,
or whatever you want to call it,
when you touch in and become that Truth,
there is no measure to what blessings you will receive.

14

Look,
if we're all one,
then it makes no sense to be a dick to your neighbor –
you might as well be fucking yourself.

And if, for some off chance that sounds appealing to you beyond the simple physical sensations, then I'm sorry to say this: that sucks.

It's not an either or kind of thing:
May we All B Blessed.

In the same way that we would tend to a wound of our body,
so we should care for other's well-fare:
that does not mean unreservedly supporting their laziness and weaknesses,
but to uplift them in such a way that they can support themselves in a manner that is joyful and fulfilling.

You can focus on what's not right and deepen its shadows, or you can focus on what's good and feed its fire so that you can see by its light and grow from its warmth.

3rd Septenary (Olympic Magic)

15 Finding the Source	**16** Principles of Magic Elemental Energies Celestial Energies Poetic Druidic Mathematical Philosophical Hermetic Theurgic	**17** Invocation Conscious Particles Control
18 Different ways of working with Spirit's Energy.	**19** Creating our Reality	**20** Cautions
21 Dismissal		

The first three aphorisms talk about the order of things. Order can be anything from a sequence of events in time or steps to be taken.

The second three talk about finding Inner Peace and Freedom by being vigilant against all things that can trip us up.

The last aphorism reminds us of prayer's power:

"Through Self, Truth is Known"

15

Remember,
you create your reality –
and of course,
don't forget to be humble about it.

The point of invoking is to know the spirits and to awaken their energies within us to use as we wish.

Don't allow the spirits to become a crutch –
a hook,
binding you to your own ignorance.

There is a string that runs through all levels of existence,
from the super-celestial to the celestial,
and from the sublunary to the infernal.

The Energy of the Universe is there,
always present,
we need only touch in with that thread to weave our reality.

16

From the principles of magic
to the mastery of the microcosmic energies,
we now move to the macrocosmic spheres,
extending the Self to the Heavenly Realms.

I love the way The Arbatel progresses from the basic principles of the arts to working with the simplest forms of energy before moving onto the celestial, poetic, druidic, mathematical, philosophical, hermetic, and divine systems. Each progressively extending one's Self till it encompasses All.

I know where I have seen 196 before, that's how many sutras in Patanjali's yogic text.

It must be one hell of a wound to need all those stitches☺

I very much love that we are under OPHIEL's administration right now☺

17

Day
Hour
Name and with Character they are to be evoked –
called forth.

Know them by whatever means comes natural to you,
be that sight
sound
feeling
or whatever,
allow their energies to arises and connect with you.

Invoke their energies into your life.

Commune with the Intelligences,
learn from their wisdom
and embody their essences:
B-come more of yourself.

Mars
Sun
Jupiter,
the ever expanding energy.

Venus
Moon
Saturn,
the ever contracting energy.

And poor little mercury being pulled and pushed aground,
yet wise old Hermes smiles as he plays around.

I love that I'm naturally Mercurial – Thanks Great Spirit.

Conscious Particles

I believe consciousness is experienced when matter, energy, time and space are together. At the most rudimentary level, consciousness is known by movement, and through movement, patterns. Internally the most basic experience of consciousness is the attraction for or repulsion from other energies/forms. The external perception that matches with that internal sensation is to witness objects being attracted to some things and not others. At the subatomic level we can see that particles have a preference, in that, they connect with some things and not others.

As those particles bind together and grow, consciousness, just like the material and energetic alchemy that goes on in chemistry, biology, astrology and everything else in life, becomes more complex. The more entangled the inner-connections are, the more intelligent and self-aware the being.

As the ancients say, "Everything has Intelligence, but some people are just Stone DUMB☺"

Okay,
so how does this all fit in with Spirits and Forces?

They are simple energy patterns; but more refined and concentrated.

What about karma and reincarnation?

We are the living embodiment of Karma,
only,
not just from one life to another,
but a composite of many different lives living out their karma together in this body and mind.

Once an energy has fulfilled/experienced its karma,
it moves on,
being replaced by other energy patterns living out their karma.

As for death, certain conscious formations/clusters of energy remain connected, being bound by energetic knots. It is these larger clusters of energy that bring past life memories. The more powerful the cluster, the more connection one will have with that life.

Larger clusters often subsume smaller ones. This in turn helps harmonize the being, as they only have one primary consciousness.

If on the other hand there are two or more large clusters vying for control of the mind we come across issues like gender conflict, dissociation, manic, bipolar, or even multiple personalities/identities. This also explains why two or more people can believe themselves to be a reincarnation of the same person.

For instance, a modern example of this conflict can be found with the Seventeenth Karmapa candidates. The truth is, they both have a large cluster of energy from the previous Karmapa.

Now, here is the catch. If we somehow fused together both Karmapa candidates, would that in fact constitute all of the previous Karmapa's energy? No.

In fact, anyone who has any interest in the previous incarnation's teachings, who finds themselves connecting with him in some way, already has a little bit of his energy within them.

And you know what is cooler than that,
anyone who reads a little bit of his writings,
listens to one of his talks,
communes with his memories will attract more of his energy into their lives.

Energy does not die.

It shifts,
reformulates,
transforms,
but never dies.

And so,
for those who understand this Truth,
they're able to consciously invite those energies and intelligences into their lives.

And one way to do this is to learn,
to study and meditate on the different Adepts' teachings.

When we do that,
we take in their essence
their intelligence
understanding
and wisdom,

We invite their bright particles to awaken within us.

I believe in Enlightenment and Physical Well-being,
Joy and Bliss,
Giving and Receiving.

There is no separation between matter/energy/spirit, for there is a thread connecting them together: consciousness.

I believe in it all,
ghost
goblins
elves and fairies,
hard working gnomes
and lazy mermaids.

I believe in drunks,
in losers and abusers,
from drug addicts to prostitutes,
from scammers to talibaners.

I believe what I see
what I feel
and know,
be it an illusion or not,
a delusion or slop,
to doubt myself is only to cause conflict.
For as much as I am out there,
I can tell you that I am definitely in here.

And so,
what I know is through my experience,
and through my experience I have come to know what I want:
I want joy, happiness, pleasure, openness, honesty, Truth, clarity, and all those other awesome qualities that I talked about in my writings.

Back to Arbatel

Consciously make your agreements, set your intention, and then stick with them.
That builds Will
Character
Energy
and Essence,
it also lets us know the sELF:

that magical creature we call ourselves☺

Who says a grimoire has to be all serious and rigid. Lighten up people, we're in OPHIEL's Time☺

I believe in having fun.

Look, I come to ritual because it feels good. I like smoking Herb and communing with the different energies of myself and the world around me. It helps me, like training, to be like this all the time. Ritual for me is about so much more than waving a wand and painting the world. I like that too, but I also like experiencing more encompassing and fulfilling states of being.

18

I AM a Yogi Adept.

19

Do you remember what I said about attracting those particles of energy you seek and letting go of those particles of energy you don't: Do it.

20

Being an Adept is like having a list of things you don't want and a shopping cart filled with all those things you do want.

21

If you have not absorbed the spirit's energy and essence,
then avoid having it around too much.
The reason for this is that it's still something outside of you, and so, it can wreak havoc in your life if you're not careful.

Continue to evoke until you no longer need to. At that point consciously invoke what you want in life and be happy – stop making fucking excuses for why you cannot be happy right now.

When we understand that it's all ENERGY

and that it all MATTERS,
we can stop wasting TIME
by inviting Joy and Blessedness into our SPACE.

21

As for my dismissal,
I just want to thank all the energies and intelligences that have peacefully come.

Thank you for sharing.

I have grown wiser in your presence,
more thoughtful,
more in control of my lower vibrations,
more aware and clear sighted in where I want to B and where I AM.

Thank you.

May all be Blessed with Joy and Bliss.
May all be Fulfilled in Spirit and in Flesh.
May all live a Full, Healthy and Prosperous Life.
May all our lives be filled with Love, Laughter, Happiness and Beauty.

Thank you.

Blessings Be…

I invite the energies in to help me heal
to become stronger
wiser.

I call the energies into my life so that I may become more aware
energetic
powerful.

I embody the energies
and I enjoy Life:
we're here,

we might as well☺

Fourth Septenary (Hesiodiacal and Homerical Magic)

22	23	24
Physical Energies Elemental Energies Celestial Energies	Validity of Energies/Spirits	Accomplished
25	**26**	**27**
Contentment Non-attachment Listening	Warning	Centering Practicing
28		
Aligning Prayer		

Before I begin to meditate on these aphorism I would like to share with you, the reader, how important it is to process through what's going on in your life. I caution you, don't reach out to greater and more powerful levels of awareness and being without first solidifying your foundation.

One reason why we do not neglect our lower formations is that it can really mess with our life. Why would you allow water damage, cracks in the foundation, and bare electrical wiring to exist under your house.

As you enter into your rituals remember to allow the mind and its worries to float to the surface. If something bubbles up, take a moment to consciously work through it: pop it. That way, instead of repressing energies, we are actually releasing them. And if you are anything like me, you will find great power in doing so.

After calming the mental/emotional planes, the energy is stabilized and ready to be worked with. At this point it is good to still the mind, humble the heart, and open your life to the energies of the Universe/GOD/ … to flow through you – forever extending and deepening your being.

After that, one thing I find useful in my ritual meditations is to set an intention. By doing that we have a direction to move towards. Time and time again I have found this to very beneficial in accomplishing my aims. While doing that, we also remain open to whatever comes. If we are aligned with our Truth, whatever does come, will always support our endeavors.

Connect with that Voice inside:
B-come that Voice.

Merge yourself with it:
Live it.

22

We learn first the energies of these human bodies,
then of the elemental and natural world,
then the celestial.

23

And so,
the Great Question that many wrestle with has come:

Are Spirits Real?

Being Mercurial I answer Yes and I answer No.

It all depends on how you look at things.

Are there really disembodied energies out there that trigger some intelligence, be that memory, information, movement, or what-have-you? Yes.

Are they sentient without some physical form to embody?
I honestly do not know.

One thing is for certain,
when I touch in with those energies there is definitely dialog,
exchange,
expansion and growth.

That is when the different theories come into play.

Is it just psychological processes going on inside our heads
or are there real alien forces that can and do interact and influence us?

I guess one question we can ask that might shine some light upon this issue is asking what relationship energy, consciousness and matter have to do with each other, and why is space-time so important to their interactions?

Not a question I wish to unravel right now.

The point is, it's not an easy question to answer, nor in truth, might there ever really be a satisfying answer. There is just too much unknown to truly ever know. But, as some adepts have come to appreciate, it's not always about the destination and external validation, but the journey and enjoyment of Life's many Blessings.

I choose to opt out of the question all together and instead just look at/into the world as energy. At that level, there is a lot less contention.

Negative energy, no matter the name, will affect us in certain ways just as positive energy will. Choosing what energy is best suited for our purposes makes sense to me. And giving it a name so that we can connect with it, is good to.

24

"When you set your mind to it,
you can accomplish anything."

While I don't think it's possible to shot the sun out my ass,
I can still see some truth in the above quote.
One thing is for certain,
if we put in the time and energy,
our wand waving will likely be more effective.

25

Find peace and well-being within yourself
and all will be a Blessing.

Don't get caught up or give up.

Trust in yourself and your Vision,
allow it to sustain and feed you.
Allow your Vision to guide and fill you with energy/life.

Listen to the Voice within,

it will guide and protect you along the Way.

Whatever that Voice maybe,
be it some spirit
deity
energy
or psychological process,
when you've aligned that Voice with your Vision,
it will guide you towards manifesting your Dream.

26

Be-Aware of those things that lead you down dark roads,
where insatiable hunger and desire eats away at your life force,
where anger and rage burn away peace and unity,
where jealousy and vengeance chew at the soul,
where sickness and dis-ease corrupt the body,
and where darkness and ignorance rein over the mind.

The Highest Truth conceivable to MinD,
is that, somehow all this is connected:
All is 1.

Anchor your focus upon one thing,
point your Self towards the Divine,
and let these fluctuations be of little consequence,
don't let them ripple your mind.

27

Why is East about wisdom
and West about strength?

I can understand East being where the light arises,
where inspiration comes,
where darkness is dispelled –
but why is West about strength?

That's where the sun dies,

when the cold comes,
where the darkness begins,
where things pass away –
that does not sound strong to me.

Maybe that is the point.
We look to the East for Wisdom because it's there,
while we look for strength where it's not.

South for caretaking?
North for a more rigid life?

I get the North, things do get colder and more rigid there –
at least, for us Northerners:
be that in strengthening and shoring up our energies
or solidifying our System/Path.

As for caretaking,
the South is where the heat is,
where the energy is moving –
doing.

Your warmth on a cold day is definitely nurturing, and the life you give to feed and nourish us is the greatest sign of caring I know.

While this is the Arbatel's energetic alignment, I suggest shifting things around to invite deeper and more encompassing experiences of knowing, as when we shift wisdom to the West and see what comes up. The directions are not rigid, they are alive and ever shifting. Touching in with the knowledge directly rather than from static pages in a book is key. For there is no greater way to know something than to be it. And to be it, you either have to be consumed by it or have consumed it, and even then, if you are not actively seeking with eyes wide open, you might miss it all together.

Seriousness
Faith
Perseverance
Certainty
are all very important.

I would add Clarity
Knowledge
Patience/Tolerance
Understanding
Openness
Compassion
Temperance
Humbleness
Simplicity
Being untethered and free from Attachment, Jealousy, Anger and Lust
Kindness
Honesty
Balance
Focus
Awareness
and Being Joyful.

I don't know about you, but I am all about inviting more wisdom and joy into my life. I want to be Wealthy, Healthy, Happy, Joyful, Long Lived, Wise and Enlightened. I want it all, and this is the Path I'm walking to invite these things into my life.

Of course you got to watch out for these: levity, arrogance, greed, vanity, envy, impiety, and so much more. There are a lot of things that can trip us up, distract us, take us down gnarly roads. That is why we work with these practices: patience, perseverance, kindness, tranquility, and so on. By working with these qualities/characteristics we naturally distance ourselves from their opposites.

With *Patience* goes impatience.
Focus – frazzled, cloudy, unfocused, etc.
Balance – unbalance and all that comes with it
Honesty both with ourselves and the world around us – dishonesty, lying, cheating, stealing and all that stuff.
Seriousness – slacking off, disrespect, laziness, etc
Faith – fear, doubt, etc.
Perseverance invites endurance, strength, dedication – while ridding us of laziness and giving up
Clarity – fogginess, uncertainty, ambiguity, dullness, etc.
Knowledgeable – Stupidity and ignorance
Patience, Openness, Non-Judging – impatience, rigidness and close-minded, gossiper and judger
Compassion and Kindness – a fucked up life
Temperance – excessiveness, imbalance, weakness and lust

Humbleness – being a giant dick
Simplicity – complexity, clutter, excessive, chaos
Untethered from fear, attachment, jealousy, rage, expectation and depleting desires.

28

Prayer is a powerful thing/action.
It empties the self,
letting everything go so that we might be filled.

Like Moses's forty years in the desert,
I am now 40 years old.

Through the trials and tribulations of the Ten Plagues
I have climbed the twisted Tree of Life,
I have transverse the Way,
and now,
within sight of the Promise Land I give my life:
I AM hOHM.

I've kicked off my sandals and warmed myself by your Sacred Light,
O, Burning Bush,
I Inhail your Essence –
your Energy:
We R 1.

Look,
you can be however you want to be,
but I can tell you from firsthand experience,
our mind's create our reality,
and when we have fucked up minds,
we have fucked up lives.

There might be moments that appear to make it worth it, but like a beggar doing a gig for a coin or two, those good moments are still quite shitty in comparison to what can be when the mind is out of the muck and aligned with the Highest/Clearest Point of Self.

Fifth Septenary (Romane, Sibylline, and Druidic Magic)

29	30	31
Power	Now	Invocation
32	**33**	**34**
Conservation Tools	Multidimensional	Simplicity Control Practical Respectful Grateful
35		
Clear Open Discerning		

"Know the Truth"

29

Working within order invites power,
fighting against the flow cr*eate*s suffering.

Embrace Self, that most rarefied point of identity –
the last step before Unity.

There's order within the Universe;
knowing this directly gives us power to work with it –
to utilize it towards our aims.

And as always,
when we work against that order for base energies,
it inevitable causes ruin.

In other words,
"Karma Sucks."

Always align/aim yourself to that which invites joyfulness, fulfillment, wisdom, connection and all the other Blessings of Life.

When you do that,
Life just gets more awesome.

Focus on that which you seek:
see it in everything you do, think and envision;
experience it in your life and feed it so that it grows.

Give it your thoughts
actions
words
dreams.

Feed it with your time, space and energy:
give it your all,
and the All you'll B.

30

Now or Never: these are your choices.

It's Time.

Right Here and Now.

Make a decision and see it through: that is one way of solidifying the Will and making it Stronger.

Don't wait for tomorrow
or for the right conditions and signs,
don't wait for the world to catch up
or for your partner/family to understand.

Do it now,

right this moment,
in this place within space-time.

Do it right now.
Right now.

Seriously,
right now.

Stop.

Do what right now?

Bring your mind to that place and abide there –
reside there,
this is your home,
your space,
your mind and body,
this is yours to do with as you wish –
what are you going to do with it?

> Thrash it
> bash it
> feed it crappy shit,
> watch vulgar shows
> and get caught up:
> consuming and being consumed?

Sadly, that is what many do.

I pray that we're all Blessed and that we're completely Fulfilled, Whole, Joyous, Free, Prosperous, Healthy, and Long Lived while Fully Enjoying and Completely B-ing Fulfilled in All Planes, Dimensions and States of B-ing.

Focus on those things you truly want and allow them to flow into your life.
Be Blessed

At some point we have to leap,

and in leaping we fall.

Trust that you will be okay as you fall into the moment:
enjoy the ride☺

How do we invite joy into this moment?
How do we invite wealth and prosperity?
How do we love and B compassionate?
How how how how how how how?

Answer any one of these or similar questions and you'll be fully Awake to Fully In-Joy Life as it is.

Get lost like the cat watching the world pass by –
be focused like a dog staring at jerky.

It is time.
No procrastination,
no more lollygagging or waiting,
do it now.

If you are here reading these words,
than Fate is on your side.

If you practice what you are reading and philosophizing about, you'll start to truly understand what those Two-Dimensional Words on the pages mean,
in fact,
you'll come to understand them from Ten different Dimensional Planes.

Through Diligence and True Understanding of Magic,
you will accomplish your aims.

Believe That.
Trust in Yourself,
your vision,
your ability to create that vision,
and you will not miss any opportunities to manifest that vision in your life.

So then,
what is magic?

Rather than define it through any one system or tradition,
this is what it means to me.

My first attempt at defining magic was light and playful.
Then serious and grandiose.
My third attempt was a long silent pause before I asked myself the question again.
This is my fourth attempt.

Magic is that feeling when something happens that is just too much to be a coincidence.

Magic is a Hermetic Process of All Dimensions Flowing 2-Gether.

And what are these Ten Dimensions

What is before us (future)
what is behind (past)
left (female)
right (male)
above (aspirations)
below (moral compass)
within (Self)
without (Other)
Connected 2-Gether (Unity)
We R 1 (Singularity)

When every particle of your being is aligned with this Truth:
That's Singularity.

The first six brings us to Self
True-Self, not that ego <u>id</u>entity/attachment.
Attachment,
makes me think of a vacuum cleaner and all their gadgets to suck us in.

When we unite the Past and Future we get the Present

When we bind together the two, we get One.
Aspiring for it All,
we align all our actions, words, thoughts, dreams and visions to the One:
adding those together we codify our identity and call it Self –
This is Me.

Meeting others we bond 2-gether
and in connecting we become 1.

Magic to me is just another means to wake-up.

Wake-up to what?

Wake up to the World we have created.

As for the practical side of magic, it's about knowing the energies and inviting or banishing them from our lives. You can call is psychological if you like, that still fits with the Hermetic Axiom, "As Within, so Without."

There are energies outside of our energies, and when we come in contact with these very real energies, intelligences, forces, et cetera, there is an interaction.

Magic is all about working with these energies and using them as we see fit.
And it is all energy,
be it a spirit
entity
God/dess
intelligence
person
self
form
or what have you.

31

With all the knowledge and tools before you,
being present in the proper space and time,
with clarity of mind and strength of body,
we call upon the energies of those domains we wish to open.

We align our environment with those formations of energy so that, as we call the intelligences forth, they come.

We R the <u>Circle</u>: that is what being **<u>O</u>**ne is

What is this Book
Gem
and Magic Horn upon my Altar?

Some say the Book of Life is made from the Tree of Life's wood.

Some call the Gem the Philosopher's Stone,
others, the Diamond of Clarity.
I've even heard it called, "just a rock," by the ignorant.

As for the Horn,
we use it to call out to the Universe:
I'M HERE

32

Don't waste energy.
If clippers are good enough to trim the roses,
don't grab the chainsaw.

Don't be an idiot either.
If the carpet is dirty, don't go starting the lawnmower.

Use the right tool,
the right stones,
metals,
and totems to accomplish your aim.

33

Don't get caught-up seeing just in one way,
be open to the possibilities –
the many paths that lead you here.

The Universe has unlimited potential, so don't limit it with those few ideas you have regarding how things should be.

Nourish your intentions with your visions, thoughts, words and actions,
surround yourself with those energies you wish to invite,
consume and grow:
Enjoy.

34

Don't complicate things, creating layers and more layers just to unravel layers upon layers of distortions, confusions, and more.

Create a space and set the parameters –
the boundaries of your control.

Get whatever you need to feel empowered. Bring whatever tools, objects/things you need to invite the energy you want, and then call more of that energy into your life. Make sure your lower formations are not causing sickness, disease, imbalance and so forth, and don't take more than you can work with in a balanced manner.

Be respectful.
Honor those energies as yourself,
for they are part of yourself.

Be Thankful,
appreciative.
and utterly imbued with Unbounded Joy and Blissful Happiness.

35

Always align with Self by being fully present in the Body, clear in Mind and Open in Heart.
Test all energies to see what they manifest
and then invite only those energies you like.

Sixth Septenary (Pythagorical Magic)

36 Theurgy	37 Order Form Mode	38 Energy Work
39 Process Perspective Discretion	40 Mindful	41 Knowledge Understanding Wisdom
42 Contemplate Diligence Trust Openness		

"Embody the Truth"

36

Simplicity is good,
when we complicated our desires
aims
goals
intentions,
we invite more room for doubt,
resistance
confusion
distortion
conflict
and other such things.

KISS is a Great Literature gift for the Adept: **K**eep **I**t **S**imple **S**tupid.

The more moving parts,
the more pieces to the puzzle,

the more difficult it is to accomplish our aims.

Of course,
complexity does color the world,
we just want to tap into the world and understand it in the simplest, most unified way: Unity.

When an Adept Attains Unity,
Their Thought and Word Manifests Reality:
For they are Gods.

The more accomplished an Adept is,
the quicker the results.

37

It's all about Order/Place in the Scheme of Things:
Character/Form and Mode/Area of Influence/Measure

Knowing the Order of things helps us navigate the world, while understanding the Essence/Character/Quality/Form of a thing helps us know the Good.

Once that's accomplished we can get in the mood/Mode in order to get things moving.

And we know the Mode by watching,
being Aware of where the energies oscillates –
resonates:
seek to remain and replicate.

Once you know the Mode you can utilized its Form to bring about the Order you called for☺

If it supports us,
encourages and strengthens us,
if it invites joyfulness
fun
pleasure
abundance
peace

satisfaction
contentment
and all that other stuff:
that's GOOD.

If on the other hand it invites sickness
pain
suffering
hatred
anger
jealousy
rage
vengeance
lust
hunger
and all that stuff:
that's BAD.

Know the energies you work with,
are surrounded by,
cross paths and connect with;
know their energies,
and if they lead away from where you want to B,
there's no reason to hold onto them.

38

Divisions of Magic

1.

The Good, the Bad, and the Will B-hind them.

2.

There are three types of practitioners:

Those that need external tools and rituals,
those that do not need tools and rituals,

and (those that do not practice at all)[2].

When we first start working with ritual, the tools are very helpful in steadying our attention, helping us to ground, and giving us something tangible to project our inner power and belief into while we work with those things we don't quite understand.

As we continue down the Ritualistic Path two things start to happen, at least, two things happened to me: I got tired of having to lug around, set up, dust, and have to deal with all the stuff, and I started to see and understand what the tools were good for. Now I no longer need them.

Even so, I still love using incense
candles
and simple tools,
for they invite joy and meaning into my Work.

3.

Knowing the Source,
why would you choose to drink anything less?

variety?

4.

There really are clusters of energies,
particles,
spirits out there,
and ritual is a great way to touch in with them.

It's not all psychological either,
there really are energies and intelligences outside of these bodies:
if you don't believe me, go suck on a polonium-botulinum lollypop and see what happens.

In saying, these bodies and minds are a composition of specific energies, and it would be remiss to believe that these compositions are the only intelligent energies/spirits/beings out there.

5.

Look,
some people are blessed with the gift/sight,

for the rest of us,
we have to go around feeling things out,
making mistakes,
and seeing what works for us.

If you have the faith to move mountains,
awesome,
for the rest of us,
it's a slow pebble moving project/process.

6.

Personifications
Embodiments of Energy

7.

Energy particles have preferences,
what they are attracted to and repulse from,
what they chase and what they run from,
what they seek to consume or avoid experiencing.

From a human
to a horse,
an eagle
and worm,
from organelles to quarks:
consciousness is there,
for why else would it have preference for one thing over another –
have an attachment to something else?

In saying,
no matter how much we try to persuade/attract a spirit, sometimes they just don't want to have anything to do with us.

39

The thing is,
I am ready to use magic to get what I want.

Why?

Because I can.

So how to use magic?

Know the season –
the time and place,
and contemplate the Word of God,
not that ink and paper blog called a bible,
but that Living Voice/Force Within U.

Descend into yourself:
shut the five doors
clear the space/mind
Know Thy Self,
and through U'R CellF/Structure,
the World.

Be humble
respectful
thankful
appreciative
friendly
loving
giving
understanding
compassionate
and wise:
align yourself with these vibrations as you commence your rituals and meditations.

Why must we be "vigilant to discern whether" we are "born to magic?" (Peterson 79)

I guess this could be looked at in different ways:

One way, did our birth predispose us to magical workings or not?

Another way could be, do we have the inclination or not?
A third way with two forks could be
are we too logical to see it
or too gullible to care?
Still another, are we deserving?
A fifth way could be dependent on the capacity and ability one has with being present and working with the energies consciously and effectively/affectively, and then of course, there is the distinct possibility that it is all bullshit, or even worse, a hologram we project upon Life.

We ultimately come to know Truth by paying attention and observing what's there, what energies are present, how certain actions affect/effect the environment and all that's within them, and then consciously choosing one's reality based off of what you seek.

Just be aware of how the energy affects you,
for that can often shift your desire –
your direction.

And some paths,
while they might offer great pleasures and gifts in the beginning,
in the end,
they do reap their rewards.

40

How is an Adept to govern themselves?

1.

Be mindful of every thought
word
and action.
Know yourself from the inside out –
nothing hid / no shadow.

And with that knowledge,
know the consequences of your thoughts
words
and actions.

2.

Always be present and aware,
never lose sight of the Spirit,
never step out of the Flow.

Be mindful of how every energy effects/affects you,
while always keeping to the Path of the Divine –
that place of Unity and Complete Fulfillment.

Don't waver,
get distracted,
waylaid,
misdirected.

No conflict:
be that inside or out.

3.

Know what the spirit, energy, force, intelligence, form and essence invites:
is it what you want or not?

Of course,
you have to know what you want,
and that depends on your perspective,
experience,
direction,
circumstances,
and so on.

Then there is that Higher Self thing,
that's what you want to tap into.

If you're not open to that right now, at least know what invites happiness and all the other good stuff in life, and then direct yourself towards those things.

4.

Avoid getting caught up,
lost in stories:
superstitions coming from others
and egotistic jaunts within the mind.

Don't be fooled by the different sephirot-self,
each vying for its own perspective and aims.

Point always to the Source:
each action
thought
word
and vision is pointed in its direction.

Then, as you transverse/open each Sephirot
there will be less chance of getting caught up in that sphere, and more chance of reaping the benefits of having consumed and absorbed the Tree's Fruit at that level.

5.

Don't get fixated on the Powers and Gifts,
and definitely don't lose sight of your Unity to it All.

Don't worship idols,
those ideas
images
forms
concepts
beliefs you have of the Divine.

Seek the Divine within
and all will be revealed.

6.

Do not give your power over to another –
be that a salesperson or another adept,

you don't need an intermediary between you and the Universe.

Know Your Self
Know Your Power
Know Your Strength
Know Your Mind and it's Godly Potential.

7.

Put everything you got into it.

A word is a tool, as is an image.

When both dissipate, what's left, just is.

Arabic Gum

When it burns it has a subtle,
gentle,
almost ethereal essence.

As it pops and sputters,
slowly burning,
a gentle smoke rises with the smell of sugar.

41

Seek Knowledge
Understanding
Wisdom

42

Study,
Be Diligent,

Trusting,
and Open to Receive

Seventh Septenary (Apollonian Magic)

43 Complete Fulfillment	44 Adepthood	45 Master Adept
46 Great Adept	47 Qualities	48 Self
49 Caution		

A fool bases happiness on what could be or what was,
a wise person seeks happiness no matter what:

"Be Fulfilled"

43

Don't neglect the small or big things.
Be Aware and Present with it All.

Seek to Fulfilled all Domains of Your Being:
Physically
Emotionally
Mentally
Energetically
and so on.

Enjoy the Pleasures of Life.
Enjoy those moments of Bliss.
Enter into that Bliss and B In-Joy.

44

Seek to B Fully Awake in all things you do.

The difference between an ignorant person and an Adept, is that an Adept accepts responsibility for their reality, the ignorant do not.
An Adept has control over their minds:
thoughts
beliefs
conditionings
emotional responses
perceptions
choices
and so on,
all the while being fully present and aware;
it would be a miracle if the ignorant could just remember the color of the car that hit them.

*I agree with you Peterson, in note 113, when you mention the constant pressure put upon us by "advertisers, politicians, and the media in general" (91). Adding in of course, schooling and everything else bombarding us on the internet, we are constantly being attacked by external energies.

45

"The highest teaching of magic is to understand what should be accepted from an attending spirit, and what should be rejected" (Peterson 91).

When we are at that place/state from which we can paint reality with the energies around us, when we have the ability to invite outside energies into our lives and use them as we wish, that is a sign of a Great Adept.

46

Align the Body, Heart, Mind and Spirit.
Where they intersect, that is the place/point we focus on:
that's where/when True and Complete Fulfillment Abides/Arrives.

Ground Yourself in this Space/Place/State/Experience,
then Stabilize
Nourish

Strengthen
and Plant Your Seeds,
Grow Your Fruits,
Enjoy Your Life:
B In-Joy

Through Humbleness and Harmony, we minimize interaction with those energies that ripple our Minds and messes with R Energies.

47

Focused/Aimed/Concentrated/Condensed
Consistent/Unrippled
Enthusiastic/Joyful
Patient and Perseverant
Open and Attentive
Fully Present and Certain
Letting Go
and Enjoying.

These are all useful when it comes to working magic.

48

Whatever energy,
formation,
intelligence,
or spirit we connect and work with,
the True Teacher is always The Self.

49

Caution and Knowledge are Good things:
Don't be stupid.

RANDOM THOUGHTS

We are fountains within the Garden,
we need only clear the passageway for the energy to flow through.

Allow the body to align itself with the mind,
don't force or push it once it starts moving –
Trust that the Universe knows what it's doing.

I would rather spend a million dollars on one good thought
then a million different thoughts on one dollar.

Don't give doubt room to

GROW

Focus.

The mind is like a virus that worms its way into consciousness,
distorting,
then claiming control.

It's about In-viting –
being in the Flow,
not vying for it.

I see you thought,
lurking,
slinking around corners –
in shadows.

DOUBT is you name.

I C U
and put out your flame.

I am going to work my magic.
There's no shame there,
there's just focus,
trust
openness
honesty
clarity
peace
balance
and a transcendental awareness arising from within immanence.

How amazing is that?

If anything,
astrology is a trigger for self-awareness and knowledge.
Be it true or not,
we learn a lot about ourselves.

If we let the stars master our lives we are nothing but slaves,
as someone once said: "The stars rule us until we rule our stars."

A large part of working with the planets is to discover who we are and how we want to live; another part is, the gathering of energy to make it so.

Part of the work is to balance those energies in our lives that are in conflict. Starting with those energies most directly in our lives. If our relationships are messed up, then we work with those circumstances until we have balanced them. Once our immediate environment is centered, we can then begin to work with those difficult aspects within our charts. Having resolved, or at least, softened those challenging planetary aspects, we can then begin to work with each of the planets in a more balanced and powerful way.

When working with transits, work first on releasing/transforming the energies before seeking to manifest your intentions. A foolish person blindly wishes upon the lamp for a kingdom of gold, only to be granted their wish at the bottom of the sea.

One of the greatest mistakes an Adept can make is to satisfy their lower natures before having gained communion with their Higher Self.

Being an Adept is about living the work, not just doing a ritual once in a while and reading a few books.

REFERENCES

"Alchemy Works Planetary and Elemental Correspondences." Alchemy Works. Web.

"Free Birth Charts." Astrodienst. Web.

"Free Transit Chart." Astrolabe. Web.

"Incense, Resins, Herbs, Essential Oils. Frankincense Specialists." Scents of Earth. Web.

"Names of the Days of the Week." *Wikipedia.* Wikimedia Foundation. Web.

Anousen, Leonte. *Olympick Magick: A Short Guide to Summoning the Planetary Spirits of the Arbatel.* Amazon Digital Services, 2014. Kindle.

Brown, Cecil H. "Naming the Days of the Week: A Cross-Language Study of Lexical Acculturation." *Current Anthropology* Vol. 30.No. 4 (1989): 536-50. Print.

Denning, Melita, and Osborne Phillips. *Planetary Magick: Invoking and Directing the Powers of the Planets / Denning & Phillips.* Woodbury, Minn.: Llewellyn Publications, 2011. Print.

Dionysius the Areopagite: The Mystical Theology and the Celestial Hierarchies. Whitefish, MT: Kessinger, 2005. Print.

Este, Sorita. *Practical Planetary Magick: Working the Magick of the Classical Planets in the Western Mystery ...* S.l.: Avalonia, 2007. Print.

Falk, Michael. "Astronomical Names of the Days of the Week." *Journal of the Royal Astronomical Society of Canada* 93 (1999): 122-33. Print.

Houlding, Deborah "Skyscript: Astrology Pages." Skyscript. Web..

Kollerstrom, Nick. "The Metal-Planet Affinities." The Alchemy Website. Web.

Lehman, J. Lee. *The Book of Rulerships: Keywords from Classical Astrology.* West Chester, Pa., USA: Whitford, 1992. Print.

Lewy, Julius. "Neo-Babylonian Names of the Days of the Week?" *Bulletin of the American Schools of Oriental Research*: 34. Print.

References

Nettesheim, Heinrich Cornelius, and Donald Tyson. *Three Books of Occult Philosophy*. St. Paul, MN, U.S.A.: Llewellyn, 1993. Print.

Nettesheim, Heinrich Cornelius, and Stephen Skinner. *Henry Cornelius Agrippa, His Fourth Book of Occult Philosophy*. Berwick, Maine: Ibis, 2005. Print.

Peterson, Joseph. *Arbatel: Concerning the Magic of Ancients*: Lake Worth, Fla: Ibis, s009. Print.

Simms, Maria Kay. *A Time for Magick: Planetary Hours for Meditations, Rituals & Spells*. St. Paul, Minn.: Llewellyn Publications, 2001. Print.

Skinner, Stephen. *The Complete Magician's Tables*. 2nd ed. St. Paul, Minn.: Llewellyn Publications, 2006. Print.

Warnock, Christopher. *Secrets of Planetary Magic*. Iowa City, Iowa: Renaissance Astrology, 2010. Print.

Warnock, Christopher. "The Planets in Renaissance Astrology." Renaissance Astrology. Web.

INDEX

Acacia 46, 53, 82, 104, 109

Agate 53, 86, 104, 109, 121

Air 37, 40, 52, 118, 119

Alchemy 51, 53, 142

Almond 41, 46, 53

Aluminum 15, 52, 104, 117, 212, 124

Amber 30, 46, 91, 100

Amethyst 38, 110, 117

Angel 38, 40, 43, 45, 48, 50, 52

Ant 68

Antelope 97, 117, 121

ARATRON 18, 22, 23, 27, 30, 34, 43, 55, 62, 64, 88, 96,

Artemis 48

Astrology 14, 83, 102, 142, 176

Badger 51, 86, 100, 102

Balance 7, 28, 29, 65, 77, 88, 94, 114, 121, 132, 152, 176

Bark 15, 16, 28, 29, 43, 55, 111

Bay 46, 70

Believe 7, 12, 35, 65, 126, 134, 136, 137, 142, 143, 144, 145, 157, 165

Benzoin 104

BETHOR 17, 24, 28, 31, 38, 55, 88, 110

Binah 32, 42

Bison 15, 46, 90, 91, 100, 101, 110, 113, 116, 117, 121

Black 20, 23

Bliss 59, 61, 125, 143, 146, 172

Blood 46, 51, 123

Blood Root 30

Blood Stone 81, 100, 110, 117, 121, 123

Blue 55

Blue Jay 121

Boggart 105

Bull 41, 46, 48, 58, 102

Calcite 53, 104, 109, 117

Candle 20, 23, 33, 45, 55, 95, 126

Carnelian 53, 101

Cedar 30, 38, 46, 55, 110

Censor 31, 55

Chanting 26

Chesed 32, 37

Chokmah 32

Cinnamon 30, 46, 71, 91

Citrine 46, 100, 117

Cloves 55

Copper 15, 39, 58, 91, 117, 121, 124

Courage 26, 51, 77, 78, 121

Crab 41, 48, 97

Crow 43, 51, 62, 66

Dance 127

Death,13, 42, 44, 62, 63, 66, 81, 113, 124, 132, 142,

Diamond 38, 43, 95, 160

Diligent 9, 38, 171

Divine 7, 9, 33, 66, 99, 131, 134, 135, 140, 150, 169, 170

Doubt 44, 62, 63, 99, 132, 136, 137, 144, 152, 162, 175, 176

Dove 41, 48, 86, 121

Dragon's Blood 32, 50, 100, 110

Eagle 38, 46, 86, 166

Earth 18, 32, 37, 40, 42, 44, 47, 50, 52, 105, 112, 118, 119, 131

East 118, 150, 151

Ego 5, 75, 125, 132, 136, 158

Elemental 5, 8, 24, 25, 98, 139, 147, 148

Elk 38, 55, 117

Emerald,40, 58, 91, 117, 121

Endurance, 44, 77, 115, 152

Eucalyptus 41, 48, 104

Evoke 93, 145

Eye (Iye) 19, 20, 21, 23, 46, 85, 117, 123

Fire 25, 45, 49, 50, 77, 79, 81, 91, 111, 138

Focus 7, 17, 22, 27, 29, 67, 84, 89, 113, 123, 125, 126, 127, 130, 132, 135, 136, 138, 150, 152, 155, 156, 173, 175, 176

Fox 53, 86, 104, 105, 116, 120

Frankincense 32, 46, 100

Fulfillment 9, 61, 76, 80, 93, 103, 108, 109, 124, 131, 136, 155, 172, 173

Garlic 50, 100

Garnet 43, 50, 110, 115

Geburah 32, 49

Generosity 44

Goetic 85, 87, 98, 106

Gold 15, 44, 46, 124, 177

Grounded 64, 67, 129

HAGITH, 21, 30, 40, 55, 58, 59, 61, 90

Hair 40, 60

Hand 17, 22, 27, 31, 112, 116, 117

Hawk 46, 51, 110, 112, 113, 116

Heal[ing] 24, 41, 70, 78, 115, 124, 146

Heart 21, 22, 26, 32, 46, 86, 98, 105, 117, 122, 147, 161, 173

Heron 73

Heaven 65, 69, 103

Hermes 53, 87, 141

Hod 32, 52

Honest[y] 46, 144, 152, 176

Image[s] 18, 57, 77, 88, 90, 102, 170, 171

Incense 11, 17, 23, 27, 28, 29, 31, 33, 57, 67, 91, 105, 109, 117, 121, 122, 165

Intelligences 6, 9, 15, 27, 28, 33, 35, 56, 93, 107, 133, 141, 143, 146, 159, 160, 165

Intention 16, 17, 20, 33, 34, 60, 67, 74, 106, 115, 122, 127, 144, 147

Invoke/Invocation 8, 34, 36, 93, 94, 131, 139, 141, 145, 154

Jade 40, 60, 117, 119

Joy 21, 29, 41, 56, 59, 60, 89, 92, 121, 125, 130, 132, 133, 143, 144, 146, 152, 157, 161, 165, 172, 174

Jupiter 11, 12, 13, 14, 30, 37, 79, 82, 88, 89, 94, 98, 121, 141

Kether 7, 32

Knowledge 5, 7, 9, 35, 53, 57, 58, 61, 66, 89, 95, 102, 106, 108, 134, 137, 151, 159, 162, 168, 171, 174, 176

Lapis lazuli 38, 55, 110, 121, 123

Larch 53, 111

Lavender 30, 53, 82, 104

Lead 15, 42, 62, 97, 117, 121, 124, 129, 150, 161, 164

Listen 7, 8, 16, 33, 73, 92, 96, 134, 137, 150

Love 7, 26, 2941, 49, 66, 71, 73, 100, 102, 109, 112, 124, 127, 129, 133, 140, 141, 146, 157, 165

Malkut 7, 32, 130, 136

Mantra[s] 11, 21- 27

Marjoram 38, 53, 56, 82

Mars 11, 12, 14, 30, 31, 32, 49, 79, 86, 94, 98, 100, 101, 111, 112, 115, 117, 121, 141

Memory 72, 106, 111, 148

Mental 16, 23, 25, 26, 36, 54, 56, 94, 106, 107, 147

Mercury 11, 12, 14, 30, 52, 79, 82, 83, 85, 94, 98, 105, 112, 116, 121, 141

Mindful 9, 162, 168, 169

Mint 38

Moon 11, 12, 14, 30, 47, 73, 94, 97, 98, 105, 117, 121, 141

Mother of pearl 48, 104, 109, 121, 123

Mouse 43, 46, 48, 86

Myrrh 30, 43, 48, 97, 104

Netzach 32, 39

North 100, 101, 110, 118, 151

Oak 30, 38, 43, 55

Obsidian 43, 62, 66, 97, 117, 121

OCH 24, 45, 55, 61, 79, 90, 99

Openness 7, 144, 152, 153, 162, 176

OPHIEL 26, 27, 52, 55, 81, 103, 105

Orange 53, 83, 110

Passion flower 30, 51, 59

Patience 7, 61, 63, 73, 103, 130, 152, 153

Pepper 30, 38, 50, 77, 100

Perspective 9, 81, 82, 111, 113, 134, 162, 168, 169, 170

Pewen 32, 50, 100, 110

PHALEG 25, 26, 31, 50, 55, 77, 99, 110

PHUL 24, 47, 55, 72, 77, 96, 103

Physical 8, 16, 17, 25, 32, 36, 58, 65, 76, 83, 99, 107, 138, 143, 147, 148

Pine 20, 23, 30, 34, 43, 50, 62, 97

Planet's Root Number 14, 37, 40, 42, 45, 47, 50, 52

Poppy 43, 48, 72, 97

Prairie dog 113

Psychological 36, 83, 94, 107, 149, 150, 159, 165

Purification 46

Quartz 117

Rabbit 41, 48, 58, 61, 73, 86, 90, 104, 116, 121

Red 50, 104, 110, 111, 113

Root 97, 98, 136

Rose 30, 41, 58, 91

Rose Quarz 40, 58, 91, 117

Sacred 57, 57, 70, 73, 92, 127, 153

Salt[y] 38, 94

Sapphire 38, 43

Saturn 11, 12, 13, 14, 30, 31, 34, 42, 43, 62, 63, 64, 65, 68, 82, 89, 94, 97, 121, 141

Sea 48, 72, 73, 74, 75, 177

Selenite 48, 97, 104, 105

Self 5, 7, 8, 9, 33, 39, 41, 42, 44, 46, 47, 49, 51, 58, 62, 64, 71, 78, 91, 97, 99, 105, 108, 117, 125, 129, 131, 132, 133, 136, 137, 139, 140, 142, 144, 150, 153, 154, 158, 159, 161, 167, 169, 170, 172, 174, 176, 177

Sigils 11-21, 27, 56, 97, 105, 117, 121

Silver 15, 17, 47, 48, 56, 74, 97, 104, 117, 121, 124

Skunk 86

Sky 105, 106, 131

Snail 73

Snake 113

South 118, 151

Squirrel 113

Steel 15, 49, 101, 110, 117, 121,

Strength 26, 46, 49, 51, 77, 78, 81, 103, 115, 121, 150, 151, 152, 160, 170

Sun 11, 12, 13, 14, 30, 44, 45, 46, 70, 72, 75, 86, 91,92, 94, 98, 101, 109, 117, 122, 124, 141, 149

Theurgia/Theurgy 5, 9, 24, 32, 129, 162

Tin 13, 37, 55, 110, 117, 121, 124

Tiphareth 7, 14, 32, 45, 130, 136

Topaz 38, 46, 53, 55, 91, 121, 123

Totem[ic] 33, 58, 114, 119, 136, 160

Tree 15, 32, 38, 50, 57, 63, 69, 70, 71, 89, 130, 131, 153, 160

Trunk 86

Turtle 73, 135

Venus11, 12, 13, 14, 30, 31, 39, 40, 41, 82, 86, 92, 94, 98, 109, 117, 121, 141

Vulture 51, 81, 100, 102, 110, 112, 113

Water 15, 37, 40, 47, 52, 71, 147

West 118, 150, 151

White 48

Willow 30, 34, 38, 41, 43, 48, 62

Wisdom 17, 18, 35, 46, 56, 57, 58, 59, 62, 64, 66, 82, 89, 92, 95, 103, 106, 124, 134, 135, 141, 143, 150, 151, 152, 155, 162, 171

Woodpecker 51, 81, 110, 112, 113, 114, 121

Worm 86, 166

Wormwood 50, 106

Yesod 32, 47

ABOUT THE AUTHOR

Some influences in Suba's life are the Grimoire Traditions, Kabbalah, Golden Dawn, Astrology, Tarot, Yoga, Meditation, Qi Gong, Martial Arts, Taijiquan, Herbalism, Buddhism, Shamanism, Babylonian Magic, Christianity, Taoism, Witchcraft, Wicca, Philosophy with a strong emphasis on Conscious Studies, Natural and Psychological Sciences, and a host of other systems and traditions.

The grimoires Suba has worked with are *The Greater and Lesser Keys of Solomon*, Eliphaz Levi's Elemental Calls, *Armadel*, *Arbatel*, *Turiel*, *Picatrix* (the lunar mansion part), *Dr. Fian's Spellbook*, *The Stone Missal*, and the systems he created.

Suba lives in the Evergreen State with his wife and little ones. He enjoys playing in the woods, swimming in rivers, meditating and doing ritual, connecting with energies, communing with Mother Earth and Father Sky, growing food for his family and friends, jumping in the leaves, and thoroughly enjoying all the Blessings of Life.

Visit www.sohmpublishing.com to learn more…

www.ingramcontent.com/pod-product-compliance
Lightning Source LLC
Chambersburg PA
CBHW081456040426
42446CB00016B/3266
* 9 7 8 0 9 8 5 1 6 7 2 6 4 *